Trying To Fit A ROUND PENIS Into A SQUARE VAGINA

"RED FLAGS" EDITION

Pre-Marital Reference Guide For Men

A. LAMAR

Copyright © 2024
All rights reserved.

No part of this publication may be reproduced, distributed, or transmitted in any form or by any means, including photocopying, recording, or other electronic or mechanical methods, without the prior written permission from the author. It is illegal to photocopy this book, post to a website, or distribute without written permission from the author.

Published 2024 ISBN: 979-8-218-42728-3

The purpose of this book is to promote self awareness. It is not intended to diagnose, prescribe, or treat any medical, psychological, physical, emotional, or medical condition. Always seek the advice of your physician or other qualified health care provider. Never disregard professional medical advice or delay in seeking it because of something you have read in this book. The author assumes no responsibility for errors, omissions, or contrary interpretations of the subject matter herein.

To My Dear Son,
For Your Unwavering Love And
Ability To See The Sun Despite
The Many Rainy Days.

TABLE OF CONTENTS

	INTRO	
1	SINGLE-PARENT HOUSEHOLD	1
2	BAD RELATIONSHIP WITH PARENTS	5
3	HISTORY OF BAD RELATIONSHIPS	9
4	NUMEROUS SEX PARTNERS	13
5	DIVORCED	17
6	CHILDREN WITH OTHER MEN	21
7	DATED A MARRIED MAN	25
8	SEXUAL EARLY IN RELATIONSHIPS	29
9	CHEATING IN PREVIOUS RELATIONSHIP	33
10	TRAUMA AND ABUSE	37
11	PREVIOUS HOMOSEXUAL ACTIVITY	41
12	LOW OR NO INCOME	45
13	PHYSICALLY OR MENTALLY UNHEALTHY	49
14	AN UNKEMPT HOUSE	53
15	DIFFERING BELIEFS	57
16	POLICE RECORD	61
17	BAD CREDIT	65
18	NARCISSISTIC BEHAVIOR	69
19	DOESN'T RESPECT HEADSHIP	75
20	LIKES MALE ATTENTION	79
21	TOO CAREER ORIENTED	83
22	AN ONLY CHILD	87
23	UNDER THE AGE OF 26	91
24	DRINKING AND DRUGS	95
25	OBSESSED WITH APPEARANCE	101
26	SUMMARY	105
	STEPS FOR SUCCESS	107

MARITAL ASSESSMENT RISK SCORE

In each chapter, the risk scale serves as a vital tool for assessing the potential hazards associated with the specific Red Flag characteristic outlined. By systematically evaluating the behavior against this scale, it provides a comprehensive understanding of the level of risk posed. Ranging from low to very high, the scale offers a nuanced perspective, considering factors such as frequency, severity, and potential consequences. This assessment aids in prioritizing interventions and implementing preventive measures tailored to mitigate the identified risks effectively.

VERY LOW

LOW

MODERATE

HIGH

VERY HIGH

INTRO

In modern times, marriage is often viewed as a potentially temporary arrangement. However, it can endure a lifetime if approached with the right mindset and partner. Most men aspire to have a wife who is supportive, caring, and respectful. Unfortunately, these qualities can be veiled until after the vows are exchanged, leaving a man to awaken to the reality that his partner lacks the basic traits essential to sustaining a thriving marital arrangement.

Navigating through this veil of uncertainty crafted by a prospective wife is challenging. The question arises: How can a man discern the true nature of the woman he is interested in? Without experience or a guide, it's impossible. And if a man chooses wrong, he can expect a relationship with constant conflict, dissatisfaction, and possibly even divorce. Moreover, selecting an unsuitable partner can hinder personal growth and prevent one from reaching one's full potential.

This relationship reference guide is specifically tailored to aid men in traversing the intricate process of partner selection. It provides crucial insights into identifying characteristics in women that may signal incompatibility, future difficulties, divorce and a host of other negative life altering decisions. While these recommendations may vary for each individual, the underlying principles serve as a compass to alert men of "Red Flags" and the defining principles behind them.

"SOME WOMEN MAY JUSTIFY THIS AS A NORM, BUT LATER REPEAT THE PATTERN WHEN THEY BECOME PARENTS."

ROUND PENIS | SQUARE VAGINA

CHAPTER 1
SINGLE-PARENT HOUSEHOLD

When you think of children's first role models, who come to mind?
Mom and Dad.

Unfortunately, single-parent households are trending upward, and when one or both parents are absent in a child's life, it usually significantly impacts the child's perception of what a healthy, fulfilled childhood is. The absence or limited access to one or both of the parents creates an undeniable void in their life that is extremely difficult to overcome, and being deprived of witnessing a thriving marriage at home may result in a woman who finds herself at a disadvantage when attempting to become a wife and mother.

As a result, the lack of a healthy, real-to-life blueprint can manifest in various negative behaviors and patterns.

WOMEN RAISED BY A SINGLE PARENT MAY

- Experience uncertainty and insecurity in relationships due to the lack of a healthy relationship demonstrated at home during their formative years.

- Lack the understanding and viewpoint on traditional gender roles and expectations within marriage.

- Struggle with their self-worth (i.e., the value placed in the self and beliefs regarding how one should be treated) and self-esteem (i.e., positive attitude about the self).

- Develop different attachment styles, such as anxiousness or aggressiveness, which can influence their approach to intimacy and communication in a marriage.

It is possible for a woman to have seen healthy marriages and effective parenting outside of her own childhood home through other family or friends. However, not having personal experience with her own mother and father can have a lasting emotional impact. Just witnessing a flourishing two-parent household elsewhere might not be enough in some cases.

Mom and Dad are usually the most important adults in a child's life, so when either fails at their role, the perceived abandonment experienced by the daughter can be a lifelong hurdle to overcome. It often causes resentment, jealousy, and trust issues.

"When Mom or Dad has not consistently provided the support a girl needs, can anyone be trusted?"

This is the message some girls receive when one parent is void, and this message can follow them into relationships they have later in life. If a woman feels that she cannot trust the object of her affection, this can potentially manifest in either one of two unhealthy extremes:

A need to have complete control over every aspect of the relationship.

A feeling of helplessness causes her to frequently worry about being abandoned by her partner, and often, this behavior is expressed by her self-sabotaging the relationship as she perceives it would end anyway.

CHILDREN

The cycle of single parenthood can often perpetuate itself, particularly among women raised in single-parent homes. Growing up without a two-parent household impacts one's understanding of family dynamics, commitment, and relationship skills. As a result, some women may justify this as a norm, but later repeat the pattern when they become parents.

CONCLUSION

Of course, I would never say that all women from single-parent households cannot become good wives or mothers, nor is it to say that all who are raised this way are destined for low self-esteem, identity struggles, and relationship dissatisfaction. However, history has shown that the majority of women raised under such circumstances experience more hurdles in trying to successfully navigate marriage and parenthood than those who grew up witnessing a thriving partnership firsthand as children.

"WHEN MOM OR DAD HAS NOT CONSISTENTLY PROVIDED THE SUPPORT A GIRL NEEDS, CAN ANYONE BE TRUSTED?"

A. LAMAR

"A LACK OF RESPECT FOR A PARENTAL FIGURE IS USUALLY A PRELUDE TO THE FUTURE RESPECT SHE WILL SHOW TO THOSE WHO ARE IN A POSITION OF AUTHORITY."

CHAPTER 2
BAD RELATIONSHIP WITH PARENTS

What happens when a woman has a bad relationship with the people who brought her into this world? Likely, everything could be better.

The primary responsibility of parents is to ensure their children's well-being for a bare minimum of 18 years. But the job doesn't end there, nor should the relationship. Ideally, parents should continue to provide emotional support, love, and wisdom to adult children in ways no one else can. Consequently, when a woman lacks a good relationship with her parents, she misses out on a significant support system, particularly when she embarks on the journey of marriage and motherhood.

Let's take a closer look at just a few of the struggles a woman lacking the support of her parents may be dealing with.

RESPECT FOR AUTHORITY

During their teenage years, some girls show a lack respect towards their parents. This can have a lasting negative impact on future relationship. While some may view their parents as overly restrictive, in reality, their parents are usually trying to protect them. Unfortunately, many teenagers rebel and break the trust with their parents, changing the relationship dynamics forever. A lack of respect for a parental figure is usually a prelude to the future respect she will show to those who are in a position of headship.

UNRESOLVED EMOTIONAL WOUNDS

If a woman's relationship with her parents, which is considered one of the most important relationships, makes her feel undervalued, she may carry the emotional burden of feeling undervalued into other relationships. She might exhibit behaviors such as seeking attention through achievement or may withdraw socially to protect herself from further emotional pain. In future relationships, some may gravitate towards partners who replicate familiar dynamics of neglect or undervaluation, perpetuating a cycle of emotional turmoil.

STRUGGLES WITH COMMUNICATION

Healthy communication patterns begin at home, and parents play a crucial role in ensuring that their children learn how to communicate effectively. When girls feel ignored or unheard at home, it can lead to lifelong difficulties in expressing themselves. An unheard girl may grow up to believe that her thoughts and feelings are not important, making it challenging for her to communicate effectively with others. In a marriage, this can result in suppressed emotions that don't get expressed to her spouse, leading to misunderstandings and resentment from both parties.

COMPLICATED NUCLEAR FAMILY AND EXTENDED FAMILY DYNAMICS

Women who have troubled relationships with their parents may try to find the emotional support they need in a romantic partner. However, expecting a spouse to fill the void left by an absent or unsupportive parent will lead to further issues. While a solid marital bond is essential, it is also crucial to maintain healthy familial relationships. Relying solely on a spouse for emotional support can lead to burnout and strain the relationship.

Additionally, women who lacks a good relationship with her parents may cause her children to inherit the same dysfunction. Her animosity can force the children to grow up without grandparents, consequently missing the love and support grandparents can provide.

Sometimes, a woman's troubled relationship with her parents can result in her being estranged from other family members, such as siblings, aunts, and uncles. As a result, her husband and children can miss out on the joys of the extended family unit. Occasions when the family gathers together may be stressful and strained relationships with extended family members can cause discomfort and issues within a marriage, particularly with in-laws.

TRUST ISSUES

Women who can't trust the people who should have had their backs will undoubtedly be slow to trust or possibly never trust completely. Trust is necessary for marriage; without it, the relationship will always lack the glue to form the deep connections needed for a thriving relationship.

STRUGGLES WITH EFFICIENT PARENTING

A woman who has a bad relationship with her parents is at an increased risk of having bad relationships with her children. She may exhibit excessive behavior to foster a positive relationship with her children, or she may risk internalizing negative patterns, leading to a destructive cycle that is tough to overcome.

LACKING CONFLICT RESOLUTION SKILLS

Just as healthy communication starts at home, learning to resolve conflict begins at home, too. A woman who has never learned to resolve the conflict she has with her parents may always lack the skills needed to navigate disagreements. Regardless of who is to blame between the parents and child, the inability to smooth things over may be replicated within a marriage when conflict arises. If a woman can hold a grudge against her parents, she definitely can keep one against anyone else.

CONCLUSION

It can be challenging for any woman who is struggling with issues related to her relationship with her parents. When a woman has a sour and estranged relationship with her parents for an extended period, it becomes her norm. She may not even be aware of how much the dysfunction is affecting her and her family. Deciding what to do in such situations demands humility, resilience, and forgiveness. A man would want his wife to have such characteristics, even if she has been wronged. Overcoming the emotional baggage requires a lot of effort; unfortunately, not every woman is suited to meet this challenge.

"THE EMOTIONAL BAGGAGE A WOMAN MAY CARRY FROM A FEW BAD RELATIONSHIPS CAN BECOME A WOUND SO DEEP THAT NEITHER A NEW PARTNER NOR TIME CAN HEAL IT."

CHAPTER 3
HISTORY OF BAD RELATIONSHIPS

Dating can be challenging, and it's not uncommon to have a few unsuccessful relationships. However, multiple unsuccessful relationships may signal "RED FLAGS" and some underlying issues that a man would want to consider.

Courting a woman with a history of unsuccessful relationships can be difficult due to the following factors.

POOR COPING SKILLS

When a woman has dealt with too many relationships that went sour, she may have developed coping strategies to help her through. Unfortunately, the coping strategy that served her well in poor relationships may not be conducive to a healthy relationship. Yet, due to her history, those coping skills may be all she knows and all she depends on. As a result, her ability to cope with relationship dissatisfaction in a way that leads to resolution and improvement may be missing.

INABILITY TO TRUST MEN

A woman who has had her trust betrayed may find it difficult to trust others. Her personal experiences may lead her to believe that men are generally untrustworthy and getting married may not change her beliefs. Even if her partner is devoted and reliable, her past experiences may make her doubtful of his intentions. This strain on the relationship may cause her partner to feel insulted and resentful.

HER DIFFICULTY OPENING-UP

Sharing emotions and being vulnerable is a vital aspect of any relationship. However, if a woman has been emotionally hurt she may find it difficult to trust and open up to a new partner. This emotional barrier can make it challenging to form a deep emotional connection with her, which is essential for building a successful relationship.

UNHEALED EMOTIONAL WOUNDS

There are not many things that leave behind a wound stronger than heartbreak. When repeated offenses of heartbreak have occurred, it's hard for most people to recover. The emotional baggage a woman may carry from a few bad relationships can become a wound so deep that neither a new partner nor time can heal it. Her emotional well-being will suffer, taking a toll on any subsequent relationships.

CONSTANT NEED TO COMPARE

Women often find themselves naturally comparing their current relationships to past experiences, yet a history of numerous past partners may foster unrealistic expectations, potentially harming the health of the relationship, particularly if these comparisons focus on negative traits. Unconsciously attributing one man's behavior to all men can occur, leading to unfair generalizations.

HER FEAR OF COMMITMENT

Repeated relationship failures can lead to serious commitment issues and a constant expectation of failure. Consequently, when negative situations arise, one may believe that the relationship is doomed and may unconsciously sabotage it before it has a chance to succeed.

HER LOW SELF-ESTEEM

A difficult failed relationship may cause a woman to reason that something is wrong with her. Women harboring these thoughts may internalize feelings of inadequacy that they cannot shake, no matter who she is in a relationship with. The key to healthy self-esteem is right there in the term, self. Even a man with the best intentions will not be able to restore a woman's self-esteem if her troubled past has too strong of a hold on her.

DIFFICULTY RESOLVING CONFLICT

A woman who is consistently in unhealthy relationships needs to consider the common denominator: *Herself*. If she repeatedly fails to maintain healthy relationships, it may indicate she cannot handle conflict effectively. Unfortunately, women who have experienced conflictual relationships can sometimes fall into a pattern of normalizing that behavior. Used to constant friction, they might view arguments and tension as the default mode of communication. This can lead them to unconsciously choose conflict over peaceful discussion, creating a cycle of negativity in future relationships.

CONCLUSION

While previous relationship experiences are not a definitive indicator of the success of a future marriage, having several bad relationships may signal that a woman is used to being unhappy in her relationships. If a woman is accustomed to unsatisfying relationships, she may unconsciously sabotage any relationship she enters. Her belief that "everything always goes wrong" can become a self-fulfilling prophecy, where her expectations become her reality.

"THE HIGHER A WOMAN'S BODY COUNT, THE MORE LIKELY IT IS TO LEAD TO COMPLICATIONS IN A COMMITED RELATIONSHIP."

Chapter 4
NUMEROUS SEX PARTNERS

Just as too many failed relationships in a woman's past can be a red flag, too many previous sexual partners are a double "Red Flag". Marriage along with the sexual component should be considered one of the most sacred aspects of a relationship. With this in mind, there is reason to be concerned when a woman has a cavalier attitude toward intimacy that she has frequently shared with numerous others.

Here are some of the concerns that may arise.

JEALOUSY AND INSECURITY

A woman's extensive history with numerous sexual partners can shatter her current partner's peace of mind. When a man knows the object of his affection has been sexual with many others before him, he must be prepared for jealousy and insecurity to rear their heads. This alone can make a man worry that he is not enough for her. These feelings may cause him to be untrusting, especially when others she has been sexual with are in her presence.

DISEASES

Women who have had numerous sexual encounters are at a higher risk of contracting diseases that could potentially endanger their health and life. A man's life is also at risk if he doesn't take responsibility and verify she is disease and infection-free. It is crucial to be aware of a woman's sexual history to avoid dealing with sexually transmitted infections and diseases. Taking responsibility for one's sexual health is of utmost importance, particularly when you're involved with a woman who has had multiple sex partners.

COMPARISON

It can be a sensitive issue for a man to think that his partner is comparing his sexual performance to that of her past partners. A woman who has had many sexual experiences with different men may have developed preferences that reflect her past encounters. For example, her new partner may be more reserved in bed, while she may have a more adventurous side. As a result, her current partner may worry about whether he can satisfy her sexually, which can further exacerbate his insecurities. Such thoughts and worries are not conducive to a healthy and fulfilling relationship.

SOCIAL STIGMA

Over time, societal attitudes towards sexual activity have become more permissive. Nevertheless, society continues to negatively judge women who engage in sexual activities with multiple partners. This type of judgment negatively affects the woman and her partner. It is unlikely that any man would feel comfortable with his significant other being scrutinized based on her sexual past. Maintaining this type of relationship can be challenging when it is constantly being undermined by rumors, whispers, and gossip surrounding the woman's sexual history. This persistent negative perception can strain the relationship and even cause it to fail. Moreover, the stigma attached to a woman's sexual history can lead to discrimination and mistreatment in other areas of life, such as employment or social interactions.

COMMUNICATION BARRIERS

It is essential for a man who is looking for a potential wife to be aware of the woman's sexual history before committing to a long-term relationship. However, some women may feel embarrassed or uncomfortable discussing their past experiences, especially if they have grown attached to their partner.

If a woman is reluctant to have this conversation, it could be an indication of embarrassment, insecurity, or deception. Therefore, it is vital for a man to exercise caution and avoid making a long-term commitment if a woman withholds this relevant information, given the high level of risk involved.

JUDGMENT WITHIN THE RELATIONSHIP

If a woman's sexual history makes her partner uncomfortable, she may feel judged. A romantic relationship is supposed to be a safe space. If the safe space is marred by judgment, resentment will become a problem in the relationship.

Judgment can be a two-way street. If a woman feels judged for her past, she will inevitably shut down conversations pertaining to her sexual history. Even more so, if a man's past is more reserved, his original impressions of the woman may negatively change. Either way, these negative emotions can severely impair the relationship.

The higher a woman's body count, the more likely it is to lead to complications in a committed relationship. The likelihood of running into one of those ex-partners increases, and some women may choose to lie or withhold the truth to avoid any awkwardness. However, such dishonesty can cause major issues of insecurity, lack of trust, and jealousy in the relationship.

CONCLUSION

Any healthy, committed, long-term relationship is going to have to address the sexual past, no matter how uncomfortable the topic may be. The more sexual partners a woman has had, the greater the risks of being with her will be. Some risks will be emotional and psychological, while others are health concerns. Either way, engaging in a relationship with a woman who has an extensive sexual past has to be approached with caution, and a suitor needs to be prepared for how her sexual past will impact the relationship, both emotionally and physically.

"LONELINESS CAN LEAD TO 'REBOUND' RELATIONSHIPS THAT ARE NOT BASED ON LOVE."

CHAPTER 5
DIVORCED

It's important to consider that divorce can be a complex and challenging experience, bringing with it a lot of emotional weight. As such, when entering into a new relationship, it's worth being mindful of any past divorces and their potential impact on the dynamics of the relationship.

Women who have gone through multiple failed relationships and those who have been divorced often face similar emotional struggles. These can include trust issues, fear of commitment, and a reluctance to be vulnerable. However, divorce can be a more drastic and challenging situation than a non-marital breakup because it involves additional stressors such as legal proceedings, financial obligations, and parenting arrangements. As a result, the emotional burdens that come with it can be much more profound, especially if the divorce is not amicable.

Here are just a few things to consider:

EMOTIONAL UPS & DOWNS

From start to finish, divorce is a long and upsetting process that takes a toll on both parties involved. It can be challenging for a woman to truly entertain the thought of another serious relationship after going through all the hardships divorce entails.

Even if a woman does re-enter the dating scene after divorce, a new relationship will not fully overshadow her emotional struggles. She may be happy to find a new partner, but resentment, sadness, and anger toward her previous spouse may linger for some years. Anxiety induced by the fear that if things went wrong during the first marriage, there's always a chance of history repeating itself, setting the foundation for a rocky start.

STRUGGLES WITH INDEPENDENCE

Some women may struggle with their newfound independence after divorce. After having their identity linked to another person, the sudden status as a single woman may lead to overwhelming loneliness, especially if the marriage lasted for years.

For most, they often yearn for another relationship, but for the wrong reasons. Loneliness can lead to "rebound" relationships that are not based on love.

Independence can sometimes have unintended consequences, particularly for women. For some, newfound freedom can be exhilarating, like releasing a captive cat from its cage. However, entering into a new relationship too quickly after achieving independence can feel like returning that cat back to captivity, which can lead to a lack of commitment and a tendency to exit the relationship early in search of that new found freedom again.

IDENTITY REFORMATION

Marriage profoundly impacts a woman's identity, both practically and emotionally. It's no coincidence that married couples names are usually mentioned together when speaking of them. Not only does marriage bring about a new way of life, but it also entails a change in identity for most women. The divorce transition can be difficult, especially when a woman's sense of self is closely tied to her partner. Emotionally, the experience can evoke a range of feelings from liberation to a feeling of grieving. Transitioning from being a wife to being single and then back into a relationship can be an emotional journey, as each relationship is unique and has different requirements.

Many women experience profound feelings of loss, sadness, and mourning for the relationship they once cherished. Similar to grieving, they may cycle through stages of denial, anger, bargaining, depression, and eventually acceptance. The end of a marriage represents the death of not just a partnership but also of dreams, shared experiences, and a vision of the future together. This emotional journey can be trying as she grapples with the reality of her new circumstances and adjusts to life without her former spouse while trying to integrate the perspective of a new man into her life.

MONEY PROBLEMS

Divorce is an expensive process, and all parties involved suffer financially from its aftermath. Money problems can be challenging in any relationship, But they can be particularly hard for women who may face financial instability post-divorce. To alleviate this, some women may seek a relationship that helps stabilize their financial situation. However, entering into a relationship with this as the primary objective can be dangerous for any man involved. While his motive for entering the relationship might be love, that sentiment may be exploited financially, leaving him emotionally devastated.

LIVING IN THE SHADOWS OF THE EX-SPOUSE

There's a reason for the saying, "comparison is the stealer of joy." After a divorce, a woman naturally compares new suitors to her ex-spouse. Considering things went wrong with her ex-spouse, the constant comparison is unlikely to be good. Living in the shadow of the "Ex" is taxing. The actual or perceived positive or negative comparisons will create tension in the new relationship.

CHANGED PRIORITIES

Her priorities may transform once a woman has gone through the marriage and divorce cycle. She may have once aspired to marry and have children, but after experiencing it firsthand, she may re-evaluate her goals, which can be challenging for a new partner who wishes to settle down and start a family.

CONCLUSION

Divorce can be a necessary step, especially when a woman is trying to escape a toxic and abusive relationship. In such cases, divorce can have a positive impact on the woman's mental and physical well-being. However, ending a toxic relationship will also come with it's emotional baggage. If the relationship ended in a way that caused heartache and hatred, the aftermath will be uneasy and complex to work through for several years afterward.

"IF THE BIOLOGICAL FATHER DOES NOT APPROVE OF ANOTHER MAN DISCIPLINING HIS CHILDREN, THE STEPFATHER MAY FIND HIMSELF WITH LIMITED AUTHORITY IN HIS OWN HOUSEHOLD."

CHAPTER 6
CHILDREN WITH OTHER MEN

Blended families are common these days, but that doesn't mean they're easy. With the nuclear family still being the ideal standard, the most desirable way for a man to form a family is by having biological children with his wife.

When a man chooses a relationship with a woman who already has children, he may encounters difficulties integrating another man's children into the new family's routine. This can be a complicated and unfamiliar process for everyone involved. However, these are the challenges that a man embarking on the journey of becoming a stepfather may encounter.

POSITION OF IMPORTANCE

Some men may desire to be their partner's top priority, but marrying a woman with children can often place a man in a secondary role. A woman's primary focus and priority will naturally be her children. As a result, a man may feel like he is competing for attention and affection, especially as the children's needs and established routines influence the household dynamics. A man's role may be more supportive and secondary as he integrates into an already-formed family unit, where the bond between the mother and children is already established.

DEALING WITH THE BIOLOGICAL FATHER

When a woman shares custody of her children with her ex-partner, her life inevitably becomes more complex with visitation schedules and co-parenting responsibilities. These are matters to be sorted out between the biological parents, making the stepfather an outsider with little input in the matter. He must learn to strike a delicate balance between not overstepping his boundaries when the biological father is also a custodial parent of the children. The situation can become even more complicated if the woman he married has children with multiple men.

If a woman has sole custody of her children and the biological father is uninvolved, that doesn't necessarily mean things will be easier. A single mother can be set in her ways when raising her children, and friction can arise within the marriage. For instance, how will their mom react if the stepfather attempts to voice his opinions on the children's behavior? If her reaction is adverse, he has to live with that decision.

A single mother may be looking for a partner who can become a father figure to her children, especially if she has sole custody. However, there may be situations where the children do not accept a new parent easily, especially if they have grown accustom to answering only to their mother.

In rare cases, the father may be awarded sole custody of the children. This may complicate things even more so. A mother may resent being shut out of her children's lives. Furthermore, if she has children with her new partner, the elder children may feel abandoned or replaced, leading to contentious relationships with half-siblings.

HANDLING DISCIPLINE

Disciplining your children is one thing, but disciplining another man's children is a different matter. A stepfather might struggle with his role and limitations when it comes to disciplining children who are not biologically his. If he has different disciplinary norms than the biological father, it can cause conflict and confusion within the family. This is especially true if the stepfather feels unheard regarding rules and regulations already established by the biological father. Furthermore, if the biological father does not approve of another man disciplining his children, the stepfather may find himself with limited authority in his own household.

DEVELOPING A FUNCTIONAL HOUSEHOLD STRUCTURE

In most cases, when a woman and the father of her children break up, they have already established a parenting routine that worked for them. When a stepfather enters the picture after their breakup, he may struggle to adapt to rules and regulations that he didn't have a say in creating. This can be uncomfortable if the regulations don't meet his standards. For example, schedules for bedtime, chores, and dining habits may have been set previously. If he wants to set his standard of rules, this may cause tension within the home, which can be especially problematic if the mother and herchildren refuse to negotiate or compromise and are set in their ways.

If a man feels confined by someone else's rules, he may struggle to lead his household according to his liking, and his role in the children's lives may become ambiguous.

THE CHILDREN'S APPROVAL

A woman may fall out of love with her ex, but the children will still love their father. It is a delicate act for a stepfather to win his stepchildren's affection while not stepping on their biological father's toes. After all, the children did not agree to the breakup. So, while the mother may have welcomed a new man into her life, the children might not be so accepting.

FINANCIAL ISSUES

When a man decides to marry a woman with children, he must be ready to take on additional expenses that he may not have previously experienced. These expenses include providing for the children's basic needs, such as food, clothing, and shelter, as well as paying for their education, healthcare, and extracurricular activities. Additionally, the man must take responsibility for his stepchildren's emotional and social needs, which can be challenging and time-consuming. In situations where the children's biological father does not contribute to their financial support, the man usually has to take on that role. Therefore, men must be fully prepared to handle the economic aspect of caring for not just a wife but understand he has inherited a family.

CONCLUSION

It's important to understand that there are exceptions to any rule, and this applies to stepfather relationships. In some cases, a healthy relationship can exist between a stepfather and his stepchildren. However, understand that you'll often find yourself competing for your woman's time and attention, as her kids will always come first. Dealing with the children's father can also bring about tense situations and financially, supporting a family that isn't yours can be tough. If you're not ready for these responsibilities, the relationship can quickly become overwhelming.

"THIS BEHAVIOR IS OFTEN DRIVEN BY A DEEP-SEATED BELIEF THAT ONE IS UNDESERVING OF GENUINE LOVE AND RESPECT."

CHAPTER 7
DATED A MARRIED MAN

Dating a married man often involves engaging in a relationship that is built on secrecy, deception, and betrayal of trust, which can have lasting effects on the individual's attitudes towards relationships and commitment. Marrying someone with this history may raise questions about the woman's values, boundaries, and ability to engage in healthy and respectful relationships. Additionally, there may be underlying issues such as low self-esteem, poor decision-making, or a lack of moral values that contributed to her poor decision which I'll address below.

QUESTIONABLE VALUES

Dating a married man typically involves engaging in a relationship that undermines the commitment and trust inherent in marriage, potentially suggesting a lack of respect for the institution of marriage and the emotional well-being of others involved. This behavior may signal a willingness to prioritize personal desires over ethical considerations and may raise questions about the woman's integrity, honesty, and empathy towards others. Furthermore, the decision to engage in a relationship with a married man may reflect a lack of self value and a need for validation that could impact future relationship.

LOW SELF ESTEEM

When a woman has been involved with a married man, she may experience emotions such as guilt, shame, and a sense of unworthiness. This is because such a relationship involves compromising one's values and settling for a situation that may not meet all one's emotional needs.

This behavior is often driven by a deep-seated belief that one is undeserving of genuine love and respect, which can lead to a pattern of seeking validation and approval from others, even if it means neglecting one's well-being. People with low self-esteem are particularly prone to entering into emotionally harmful or unfulfilling relationships because they may not prioritize or recognize their self worth or have the confidence to assert their needs and boundaries.

POTENTIAL FOR INFIDELITY

Women who have dated a married man may face an increased risk of engaging in infidelity in future relationships. Engaging in a relationship with a married individual often involves secrecy, deception, and a breach of trust, which can desensitize individuals to unethical behavior within romantic contexts. This normalization of infidelity may lower the threshold for engaging in similar behavior in future relationships, particularly if unresolved emotional issues from the experience persist. Additionally, women who sustain such a relationship for a period of time may develop coping mechanisms such as compartmentalization or rationalization to justify their actions, making it easier to rationalize future instances of infidelity.

EMOTIONAL BAGGAGE

The secrecy and deceit inherent in such relationships can lead to feelings of inadequacy, self-doubt, and worthlessness, as individuals may struggle with reconciling their actions with their values and beliefs. Additionally, the end of such a relationship may trigger feelings of grief, rejection, and abandonment, mainly if the affair was emotionally significant. As mentioned before, these unresolved emotions can manifest in various ways, including difficulties forming trusting relationships, fear of commitment, or struggles with self-esteem and self-worth.

CONCLUSION

Entering into a relationship with a woman who has previously been involved with a married man is fraught with peril. This situation screams red flags, suggesting she may have a blatant disregard for moral boundaries and an unsettling comfort with deceit. The emotional wreckage from her past entanglement can poison your new relationship, dragging you into a web of lies and mistrust. Her history indicates a disturbing tolerance for infidelity, putting your trust and peace of mind at constant risk. Moreover, her past actions could tarnish your reputation, exposing you to social scorn and judgment. Engaging with someone who has such a questionable history is a reckless gamble, endangering your emotional well-being and integrity. It is essential to approach such situations with caution.

"ENGAGING IN A RELATIONSHIP WITH A MARRIED INDIVIDUAL OFTEN INVOLVES SECRECY, DECEPTION, AND A BREACH OF TRUST, WHICH CAN DESENSITIZE INDIVIDUALS TO UNETHICAL BEHAVIOR WITHIN ROMANTIC CONTEXTS."

"WHEN A WOMAN DOES NOT HONOR SEX AS SACRED AND FAILS TO PRIORITIZE THEIR OWN WORTH AND PHYSICAL WELL-BEING, IT IS A CAUSE FOR CONCERN."

CHAPTER 8
SEXUAL EARLY IN RELATIONSHIPS

Intimacy is an important component of any relationship, and sexual activity is traditionally seen as a sacred act reserved for sacred bonds. In today's highly sexualized culture, finding a partner who shares this view of sex may be a challenging task. However, those who find such a connection can expect a long-lasting, fulfilling, and trusting relationship.

When a woman engages in sexual activity early in a relationship, before forming a meaningful emotional bond, it may suggest that she doesn't view intimacy as something special and regards sex as a casual activity. A woman who does not value the importance of intimacy in a long-term relationship due to her cavalier attitude towards sex may not be suitable for a committed partnership.

Additionally, a woman who is lax with her body, sexually speaking, may lack a sense of self-value, which in turn begs the question of how others view her. A man may wonder, "How many other men have experienced this personal act just as fast with as little effort as I have? And, will she still be as easy with other men besides me in the future?

Beware the following concerns whenever a woman is quick to turn sexual.

RUSHED COMMITMENT

A woman who prioritizes sex at the start of a relationship may be hiding aspects of her personality she doesn't want men to see. Why? The decision to engage in sexual activity early on in a relationship may result in accelerated commitment and exclusivity without a clear understanding of the individual's true nature or identity. Hasty decisions in this regard may lead to undesired consequences that could harm a man's future. Establishing a dependable foundation of trust and communication is crucial, as a lack thereof indicates carelessness and immaturity and sometimes can even be dangerous.

MISMATCHED EXPECTATIONS

When a woman engages in sexual activity early on in a relationship, it can create unrealistic expectations regarding the pace and progression of the relationship. A woman may believe this is the best way to attract a good man. However, if her attitude towards sex is this casual, her intentions and level of commitment may be easily misinterpreted. Women in this category may have a history of one-night stands.

LIMITED FOCUS ON OTHER AREAS

Introducing sex too early in a relationship can be detrimental to other important aspects of the relationship. Engaging in a most intimate act before forming mental stimulation, emotional connections, and healthy communication patterns can cause these crucial areas to be neglected. It's important to note that sex alone cannot sustain a relationship.

REGRET

Lust can easily take over and lead a couple into engaging one another sexually early on. However, when lust subsides, and rational thinking kicks back in, feelings of guilt may creep up. One or both parties may realize they weren't emotionally ready to make the relationship sexual. But once the act has been done, it can't be taken back, and the relationship dynamics will be changed forever.

CONCLUSION

Entering into a relationship with a woman who is sexual early on is laden with serious dangers. This behavior can be a glaring "Red Flag", signaling a lack of depth and an alarming readiness to rush into physical intimacy without establishing a meaningful emotional connection. It may signal her lack of respect for her body and point to a history that might be littered with casual flings, suggesting she may have commitment issues or a propensity for infidelity. Such premature intimacy can cloud your judgment, blinding you to critical red flags and incompatibilities that will inevitably surface later.

There is reason to be cautious about this chapter when searching for a serious, long-term commitment that leads to marriage. With physical intimacy being essential to a healthy marriage, it never bodes well when a woman does not honor sex as sacred and fails to prioritize their own worth and physical well-being, it is a cause for concern.

To have a marriage with a strong bond, both emotionally and physically, it is imperative for a man to have a wife who respects herself and is willing to work on building a meaningful connection first, outside of sex.

"A WOMAN WHO PRIORITIZES SEX AT THE START OF A RELATIONSHIP MAY BE HIDING ASPECTS OF HER PERSONALITY SHE DOESN'T WANT MEN TO SEE."

"THE BEHAVIOR OFTEN STEMS FROM AN INABILITY TO BE HONEST AND UPFRONT WHEN A RELATIONSHIP HAS RUN ITS COURSE."

CHAPTER 9
CHEATING IN PREVIOUS RELATIONSHIP

Nothing can destroy a relationship like infidelity. When a romantic partner is caught cheating, the relationship is forever changed. Even if the innocent party involved leaves the relationship, the hurt and betrayal can negatively impact their future relationship for many years afterwards.

Here are some issues that can arise when a woman's previous relationship involved cheating - whether she was being cheated on or committed the cheating.

IF A WOMAN HAS BEEN BETRAYED BY CHEATING, SHE MAY

Struggle to trust new relationships due to her experience:

In the aftermath of being cheated on, a woman may be marred to the point of presuming everyone is "guilty until proven innocent." Entering the dating world again may automatically put her on guard, and new suitors may never gain her complete trust.

Insecurities and fears:

Insecurities and fear may lead to constant suspicion, over-analyzing innocent actions, and seeking reassurance from her new partner. Such behaviors can create a toxic dynamic of mistrust and suffocation within the relationship, ultimately eroding the foundation of mutual respect and understanding. Furthermore, her fear of being hurt again may cause her to preemptively withdraw emotionally or push her partner away as a defense mechanism, inadvertently sabotaging the potential for genuine connection and intimacy.

Communication:

Even if a woman finds love after an unfaithful relationship, she may feel the need to hold back with a new partner. A successful relationship requires both parties' willingness to be vulnerable with each other. Still, most women, rightly so, remain reserved, which hinders the ability to form a deep, emotional connection.

COMPARISON

Some women may have difficulty seeing a new partner for who he is rather than constantly comparing him to an ex. These comparisons may occur in attempts to identify red flags hinting at infidelity, pushing a woman to abandon a relationship before it gets too serious.

AVOIDANT ABOUT HER PAST

The anger and shame resulting from being cheated on may cause a woman to refrain from discussing her past, which in turn can make her new partner feel like she's hiding something. The secrecy can lead to unwarranted suspicion. If a woman refuses to process her past with her current partner, he may feel disconnected and confused about her feelings for him.

TRUST

Most women who have had their trust betrayed by a romantic partner will carry that heartbreak with her for a long time. Committing to a relationship with her after such an experience is understandably a challenge. Her faith in relationships can be permanently damaged, and her skepticism and lack of trust toward new partner can become a stressor.

Sometimes, however, women commit the offense. In this case, a new suitor must consider certain things for his own protection.

If a woman has cheated previously, pay attention to:

HER LOYALTY

Some find cheating a hard habit to break. The behavior often stems from an inability to be honest and upfront when a relationship has run its course. A woman who has cheated before may be the type who won't openly admit it when she is ready to move on. Therefore, trusting her can be risky.

HER SELF-ESTEEM AND RELATIONSHIP SATISFACTION

Low self-esteem, mainly if it stems from no longer feeling sufficiently desired, can be a catalyst for a woman cheating. She may seek comfort and validation outside of the relationship. If she receives the comfort and validation she craves outside of the relationship, it can become a high that she wants to hold onto, and it may eventually take precedence over her primary relationship.

REVENGE

Marrying someone who cheated for revenge sets off alarm bells for the long-term health of your relationship. Their actions demonstrate a concerning pattern: prioritizing anger and emotional manipulation over open communication and trust. This tit-for-tat resentment can be a prelude to how she resolves issues. Imagine navigating future conflicts; will they lash out with infidelity again or withhold her love emotionally as a weapon? Building a secure and fulfilling relationship requires open communication and a commitment to tackling challenges together. Revenge cheating suggests a lack of these crucial ingredients. It can signify unresolved issues in their past relationship, which could easily spill over into a future relationship. Marrying with the hope of "fixing" someone who cheated for revenge is a recipe for disappointment.

CONCLUSION

Whether a woman has been cheated on or has cheated, it is likely to affect her future relationships in some way or the other. Those situations raise "Red Flags" about her ability to maintain loyalty and her ability to trust, crucial components of any healthy relationship. The fear of being betrayed can cause immense emotional stress and insecurity, potentially leading to obsessive behaviors or conflicts. Moreover, her past actions might indicate deeper issues with commitment and honesty, suggesting a propensity for deception. Engaging with someone who has such a questionable past is a gamble, risking not only your emotional well-being but also your sense of security and peace of mind. Therefore, without undeniable proof of significant personal growth and change, the relationship is almost guaranteed leave you feeling cheated.

"PATIENCE, PERSEVERANCE, AND UNDERSTANDING ARE NECESSARY QUALITIES TO HAVE WHEN ENTERING INTO A RELATIONSHIP WITH A WOMAN WHO HAS SUFFERED FROM TRAUMA."

CHAPTER 10
TRAUMA AND ABUSE

Experiencing a traumatic event can have significant emotional and psychological repercussions that may endure for an extensive period. It is imperative to comprehend that women who have been subjected to physical or sexual abuse or any other traumatic experience are in no way accountable for what has happened to them. They should never be subjected to shame or made to feel culpable for what has transpired. When a man is courting a woman who has suffered under these circumstances, it is crucial to bear in mind that she may be grappling with various challenges, including:

SHATTERED TRUST

Sexual abuse is a heinous crime that leaves a deep and lasting impact on its victims. Women who have experienced such trauma struggle with feelings of mistrust, vulnerability, and fear. The trauma can manifest in various ways, making it challenging for them to form and maintain healthy relationships. The path to healing and recovery from such experiences is often long and arduous, requiring a great deal of patience, compassion, support from loved ones and counseling.

INTIMACY ISSUES

It is essential to consider that individuals who have experienced sexual abuse in the past may struggle with intimacy in their future relationships. Even when in a loving and consensual relationship, survivors of abuse may encounter physical intimacy issues due to specific actions that trigger traumatic memories. At times, these individuals may feel discomfort and reflexively push their partner away. A man would need to have a high level of empathy and patience.

IMPAIRED PHYSICAL HEALTH

Sometimes, trauma impairs physical health. The aftermath of sexual abuse can manifest in physical challenges for a survivor. Chronic pain, particularly in the pelvic region, is a common issue. This can make intimacy difficult or even painful. She might also experience digestive problems, sleep disturbances, and tension headaches. Understanding and patience are crucial. Respecting her boundaries and open communication are key. A supportive partner can help her explore treatment options and would have to create a safe, comfortable space for intimacy to develop at her pace.

EMOTIONAL INSTABILITY

Women who've been traumatized or abused may have a host of triggers, some of which they may not even be consciously aware of, which can lead to mood swings, anxiety, depression, and PTSD, which may sometime manifest in low self-esteem that can hinder a woman's ability to fully engage in relationships, even when a man has good intentions.

AVOIDANCE

Sometimes, women are aware of their triggers. Hence, they may avoid specific locations, situations, and topics. Avoidance can make loved ones feel rejected if they do not understand how the abuse survivor copes emotionally and psychologically for her protection and well-being.

FEAR OF VULNERABILITY

Trauma and abuse forces a woman to feel vulnerable in the worst way. As a result, a fear of vulnerability can develop. A woman may feel the need to be strong, distant, or detached from others simply as a way to protect herself from the chances of future abuse.

MALADAPTIVE COMMUNICATION

Being dismissed or invalidated can intensify feelings of shame, self-blame, and worthlessness, compounding the already deep-seated wounds inflicted by the abuse. The lack of acknowledgment or support can intensify feelings of isolation and alienation, leaving her to grapple with her pain in silence. As her experiences are minimized or brushed aside, she may internalize a sense of powerlessness and hopelessness, doubting her own perceptions and diminishing her ability to seek help or healing.

The dismissal can also fuel feelings of anger, resentment, and mistrust towards others. As these emotions fester unchecked, they can poison the foundation of any new relationship, leading to resentment, withdrawal, and ultimately, the erosion of intimacy and trust. She may find herself trapped in a cycle of trauma, unable to fully engage in any healthy relationship and heal from her past wounds.

RELIVING THE TRAUMA

Trauma can leave a profound impact on an individual's mental health. It can result in unexpected and distressing flashbacks, often accompanied by vivid sensory details that transport the person back to the traumatic event. These flashbacks can be triggered by a wide range of seemingly innocuous stimuli and can be difficult to manage. Nightmares are another common symptom of sexual trauma, which can leave the individual feeling fatigued and emotionally drained. Obsessive thoughts and ruminations about the traumatic experience can also be a source of great distress, constantly intruding into the person's consciousness and disrupting their daily life.

CONCLUSION

It is crucial that survivors of sexual abuse receive empathy and emotional support. While it is possible for them to have healthy and meaningful relationships, it is vital for a woman to seek counseling and for the man courting her to be prepared for the challenges that may arise. The relationship is likely to have its ups and downs as the survivor works through their trauma.

Patience, perseverance, and understanding are necessary qualities to have when entering into a relationship with a woman who has suffered from trauma or abuse. If a man lacks these qualities and is not willing to deal with the long-term aftermath that may come with it, then it may not be the right relationship for him.

"WAS IT ABOUT SEX, LIFESTYLE, OR HER NATURE?"

CHAPTER 11
PREVIOUS HOMOSEXUAL ACTIVITY

When in a relationship, it is crucial not only for both parties to be open and honest about their sexual history but about their sexual orientation as well.

In modern society, it is no longer uncommon for people in heterosexual relationships to have dabbled in homosexual activity in the past. Hence, it is possible to encounter a woman who ultimately hopes for heterosexual marriage and children at some point despite potentially harboring homosexual desires and homo-erotic interests.

If a woman secretly or occasionally desires other women, this can pose problems for a male partner who is not comfortable with sexual fluidity. The issue will arise within the relationship and can become a problem for a long-term commitment like a marriage.

Here are some of the problems that might come up.

PERCEPTION

Most men can confidently pursue a woman due to the belief that he has more to offer than the next man. However, this perception changes when dealing with a woman who has dabbled in homosexual affairs. A woman's past sexual exploration may have initially been considered a fad but no matter how you slice it, a man is not emotionally or physically the same as a woman. He's a man.

This may ultimately lead a man to wonder what caused the curiosity and willingness to enter a homosexual situation. Was it about sex, lifestyle, or her nature? More importantly, after resuming a heterosexual relationship, will she one day have another change of heart and return to a gay lifestyle?

A woman who is either fluid with her sexuality or struggling to figure it out will cause a male partner to perceive their relationship differently and reconsider the potential for longevity.

SOCIAL STIGMA

The LGBTQ community has been steadily gaining support and acceptance in society, but alternate sexualities are still taboo in some cultures. If a man is in a relationship with a woman who has previously experimented with her sexuality, the relationship could potentially face judgment if friends and family members aren't so accepting. Their attitudes can make it difficult for the couple to navigate their relationship. Furthermore, tension can develop if the woman perceives her partner as not supportive of her and unwilling to stand up for her against the judgment of others.

TRUST

A man may want to accept his partner, but often, it becomes too mentally draining to worry about the chances of another man or woman coming between them. If a man has any concerns whatsoever about his partner's loyalty, his concern will grow if his partner has bisexual tendencies.

These trust issues will put a strain on the relationship and potentially impair the relationship from progressing. If a man is bothered by his partner's sexual past and orientation, he may have to think twice about marriage and family planning with her. If her sexuality is going to be a matter that he cannot accept, a long-term relationship with her won't suit his needs. Furthermore, due to her past exploration, she will not want to be with someone who makes her feel judged or does not trust her ability to be faithful.

CONCLUSION

A man who is not comfortable with his partner's sexuality is going to find himself unable to relax and trust the relationship. Trust issues are practically inevitable, with doubts lingering about fidelity and whether you truly satisfy her needs. If you're not prepared to weather the storm of judgment and self-doubt that comes with this territory, you're in for a rough ride. Therefore, if the knowledge that a woman has lived a homosexual lifestyle or occasionally experiences same-sex attraction is worrisome, it is best to refrain from pursuing a relationship with her. The relationship will not thrive under discomfort and judgment.

"A WOMAN WHO IS EITHER FLUID WITH HER SEXUALITY OR STRUGGLING TO FIGURE IT OUT WILL CAUSE A MALE PARTNER TO PERCEIVE THEIR RELATIONSHIP DIFFERENTLY AND RECONSIDER THE POTENTIAL FOR LONGEVITY."

"SUCH AN ATTITUDE MAY CREATE A SENSE OF DEPENDENCE THAT MOTIVATES HER TO SEARCH FOR ROMANTIC RELATIONSHIPS WHERE SHE RELIES ON HER PARTNER FOR FINANCIAL SUPPORT."

CHAPTER 12
LOW OR NO INCOME

Shared values, common interests, attraction, communication, and compatibility are all important considerations when selecting a life partner. Yet another is necessary... Finances.

It's worth noting that some men may prefer their wives to stay at home rather than work. However, if a woman is not in this type of relationship and she is either not working or earning a low income, this is definitely a "Red Flag."

Let's take a closer look at why this might be the case.

CO-DEPENDENCY

Fact: A woman with low or no income often depends on others for survival. In a committed relationship, such as a marriage, this may not necessarily be a problem. However, in a new relationship, such an arrangement will create an imbalanced power dynamic that can prevent the relationship from developing organically.

LAZINESS

Laziness often keeps a woman from being gainfully employed. Laziness and co-dependency are closely linked. A lazy woman might get used to doing the minimum necessary to survive and rely on others, such as child support, government assistance, or unemployment benefits, to do the rest. Such an attitude may create a sense of dependence that motivates her to search for romantic relationships where she relies on her partner for financial support. However, this behavior may cause her partner to feel used, leading to tension in the relationship.

ENTITLEMENT

Some women aren't lazy but some women who are not self-motivated to work or pursue higher-paying employment may harbor a sense of entitlement. Rather than earning the means to provide for herself, she may feel others should provide for her. This perspective may be rooted in the individual's upbringing, mainly if they are accustomed to having everything handed to them rather than earning it themselves. A new partner will ultimately become a supporter. If the relationship progresses, a man may start to feel exploited. Especially if intimacy becomes associated with his giving. In such a scenario, it may be challenging to maintain a positive outlook on the relationship.

FINANCIAL STRAIN

If a man's primary objective is to build wealth for the future, the other party's little or lack of income will hinder this process. A woman's inability to contribute financially could lead to financial strain. A single paycheck might not suffice for homeownership, family planning, college funds, retirement savings, or unforeseen expenses. Most men will eventually become fatigued with shouldering the majority of financial obligations if their partner fails to contribute to the financial growth of their household.

LIMITED LIFESTYLE CHOICES

Travel and leisure activities are often factors that enrich a couple's lives. But when finances are strained because only one partner is able to contribute meaningfully, the couple will be limited in what they can afford to do for fun.

LOW SELF-ESTEEM OR DEPRESSION

Low self-esteem and depression are often interconnected. A woman struggling with either or both of these issues may lack the motivation and energy to pursue a career. In this case, the root cause of her low self-esteem and depression will have to be worked through before she can successfully contribute to the home financially. Once you go down this rabbit hole, it may be discovered that many other emotional factors are contributing to these emotional issues.

LACK OF EDUCATION

A woman's career advancement can be significantly impeded by the absence of higher education. Without a formal education, she may become stagnant, dissatisfied, and disinclined to pursue better-paying job opportunities. This can negatively impact her mood and well-being in the long run, especially if she remains unmotivated to find work that fulfills her.

CONCLUSION

Either of these scenarios may negatively impact a relationship. Financial strain is not the main problem, but a woman's lack of motivation and aspirations will eventually trickle down to the home physically and emotionally. Her lack of motivation may spill over into other aspects of the relationship. and caring for the home and children which can quickly become a significant source of tension and stress. A man might ultimately find that he is shouldering the bulk of these responsibilities. For this reason, a gainfully employed and motivated woman will have a better chance of helping a relationship thrive. If dealing with a low or no-income woman, be prepared for all the hardships that entails, both emotionally and financially.

"POOR HEALTH CAN SIGNIFICANTLY IMPACT THE INTIMACY OF A MARRIED COUPLE, BOTH PHYSICALLY AND EMOTIONALLY."

CHAPTER 13
PHYSICALLY OR MENTALLY UNHEALTHY

Health is wealth. Although some health issues cannot be avoided, a good quality of life can often be achieved through healthy eating habits, regular exercise, and safe choices. Regrettably, many individuals rely solely on genetics to maintain their appearance, which, as they age, proves insufficient. Poor food choices and lack of exercise can significantly deteriorate a woman's physical and mental health. Without adopting a healthy lifestyle, this deterioration is likely to continue.

Marrying a woman who is in bad health, physically or mentally, will pose many challenges, including the following.

PHYSICAL HEALTH

Being out-of-shape can lead to limited ability for certain leisure activities. Things that get taken for granted, like being able to walk without running out of breath can significantly diminish the quality of life. Relationships suffer when one party cannot join the other due to quickly growing physically exasperated. Vacations, leisure activities, and hobbies will all be affected.

DAILY FUNCTIONING CAN BECOME A PROBLEM

Lack of physical fitness can seriously impede an individual's ability to perform basic household tasks, such as cooking, cleaning, and caring for children. This can lead to an unacceptable reduction in the overall happiness of a couple, as one partner may be unable to contribute equally to household responsibilities. Furthermore, if one partner's poor health status hinders their ability to partake in household tasks, it will inevitably result in the other partner assuming an excessive amount of responsibility.

Poor health can significantly impact the intimacy of a married couple, both physically and emotionally. Chronic illnesses, physical disabilities, or mental health struggles can lead to decreased libido, pain during intimacy, or emotional distress, all of which can disrupt the couple's ability to connect intimately.

The stress and strain of managing health issues may also lead to decreased communication, feelings of frustration, or resentment, further eroding the emotional intimacy between partners.

Poor physical health can have a negative impact on mental health and create a complex relationship between the body and the mind. When the body is suffering from chronic illness, injury, or other lifestyle factors, it can lead to a range of adverse effects on mental well-being. Physical discomfort or pain can lead to frustration, anxiety, and depression, as it can prevent a person from engaging in daily activities and enjoying life. Additionally, the limitations caused by poor physical health can affect self-esteem and self-confidence, leading to feelings of inadequacy and helplessness.

MENTAL HEALTH

Forming a relationship with a woman who has mental health struggles may result in a range of challenges. The nature of the mental health issues and their severity may contribute to various fluctuations in the relationship. Such fluctuations may involve periods of heightened stress, emotional instability, strained communication, or even crises that necessitate professional intervention. A man may have to bear the financial costs of therapy and medication and find himself balancing care-giving with other responsibilities, which can be emotionally draining.

EMOTIONAL STRAIN

In a marriage, a spouses physical and mental health will emotionally affect the other. It is hard to watch a significant other struggling with health and mental issues, and coping can be exceptionally difficult.

This emotional strain can impact the mental health of both partners. Being unwell takes a toll, just as caring for the unwell. If the stress overwhelms, professional help may be necessary, which can add to financial and emotional strain.

LONG-TERM WELL-BEING CONCERNS

Whenever health becomes a concern, a man must think about his significant other's long-term well-being. When a man takes a wife, this is a lifetime commitment (For better or worse. Till Death do us part). The last thing he wants is for that lifetime to be cut short or for the quality of their lives together to be diminished by illness. Wedding vows include taking a partner in sickness and health. However, a sick partner who could have prevented their condition through better choices can sometimes leave a significant other feeling resentful.

FAMILY PLANNING CONCERNS

If a woman hasn't made her health a priority, it could be a "Red Flag" regarding family planning. Pregnancy is a challenging experience both physically and emotionally. Even women who are in perfect health can experience complications. Therefore, a woman who is not taking good care of her body may be at a higher risk of complications.

Even if the pregnancy goes smoothly, the aftermath may still be cause for concern. Recovering from the pregnancy can be a challenge, and caring for the children can be a challenge. If a woman is not healthy, her spouse may find himself as the main caregiver... Of the children and the woman.

CONCLUSION

Noting the attention a woman gives her health, both physically and mentally is essential before getting too deeply involved in the relationship. Ideally, a man should take care of his health and want a partner who prioritizes doing the same for herself. Therefore, before committing to an unhealthy woman, it is important to be aware of the potential challenges that may arise due to her unhealthiness. Failure to do so may result in long-term physical and emotional complications that could potentially cripple the future happiness of the relationship.

"THE STATE OF ONE'S LIVING ENVIRONMENT OFTEN REFLECTS THEIR HABITS, PRIORITIES, AND MINDSET."

CHAPTER 14
AN UNKEMPT HOUSE

It is significant to note that the cleanliness of one's living space reflects one's personality, habits, and mental state. Also the perception of cleanliness can vary significantly among individuals, often reflecting their upbringing and surrounding environment. A well-maintained home can signify diligence and conscientiousness. On the other hand, an unkempt home may signify a more significant issue within a persons character. A neglected home can indicate a lack of discipline and order, which usually carries over into other aspects of her life. As such, a man who is conscientious about his environment will consider the cleanliness of a woman's home.

Here's a list that may come with a woman that keeps an unkempt home.

DISCOMFORT AND STRESS

Someone more accustomed to a clean and well-maintained living space will feel uncomfortable in a messy environment. The desire for a clean household while living with someone who does not share the same values will be a source of frustration. Some people cannot mentally handle clutter and disorganization and a man who likes tidiness versus a partner's lack of cleanliness will eventually lead to a "mess" of a relationship.

The discrepancy between his expectations and the reality of the unkempt space may create tension and conflict within the relationship, as he struggles to reconcile his desire for cleanliness with the situation at hand. Additionally, the presence of clutter and messiness can disrupt his sense of tranquility and mental well-being, hindering his ability to relax and feel at ease in his own home.

A couple with different standards regarding house cleanliness is likely to experience conflict when delegating household chores. Furthermore, it is unlikely that the less tidy partner will do their share of cleaning to the other's satisfaction. This may leave the tidier partner feeling the need to clean up behind the other, doubling the workload. Household maintenance will feel imbalanced, and a man may resent his woman's inability to keep the house as he think it should be.

STATE OF MIND

One's environment reflects one's state of mind. A woman who maintains an unkempt home may signal a lack of discipline and order, which can have implications for her overall well-being and effectiveness in managing responsibilities. The state of one's living environment often reflects their habits, priorities, and mindset. Consistent disorder and clutter may indicate a tendency towards procrastination, disorganization, or a lack of attention to detail.

It also suggests a woman having difficulty in establishing routines and systems necessary for effective household management. While individual circumstances and priorities vary, a consistently unkempt home may reflect underlying challenges in prioritizing and managing tasks, which can impact various aspects of life beyond the home.

Chronic stress, depression, or feelings of overwhelm may lead to a lack of motivation or energy to maintain a tidy living space. Similarly, unresolved emotional issues or distress can manifest in clutter and disarray, mirroring the chaos within a womans emotional state of mind. For some women, an unclean house may serve as a visible expression of internal turmoil, with each untidy corner symbolizing unaddressed emotions or unmet needs.

LAZINESS

Laziness can significantly contribute to an unkempt home as it often manifests in a lack of motivation or willingness to maintain cleanliness and order. When a woman succumbs to laziness, she may neglect regular cleaning tasks, such as tidying up clutter, doing dishes, or vacuuming floors. Procrastination and a preference for comfort over effort can lead to piles of dirty laundry, unwashed dishes, and neglected chores accumulating over time. This inertia can create a cycle where the mess grows, demotivating her from addressing it. As a result, an unkempt home becomes a visible reflection of one's tendency towards laziness and reluctance to take action.

DIFFICULTY ENTERTAINING GUESTS

A man who highly values cleanliness would feel uncomfortable inviting family and friends over if his partner fails to maintain a tidy home. This discomfort could lead to the couple hosting guests less frequently, which may result in feelings of isolation or estrangement. Alternatively, if guests are invited over, the state of the home could cause embarrassment, potentially damaging a man's pride and character.

FINANCIAL PROBLEMS

In addition to posing health risks, being aesthetically unpleasing, and causing embarrassment, an unkempt house can lead to more significant financial inconveniences. An untidy person is usually an unorganized person. Bills and important documents can easily be misplaced with too much clutter. Having to pay late fees or credit score lowered because one partner disorganization will become yet another source of contention in a relationship.

CONCLUSION

Entering into a relationship with a woman who maintains an unkempt home presents several significant challenges that should be approached with careful consideration. The state of one's living environment can have notable impacts on both physical and mental well-being. Living in a consistently disorganized and unclean space can contribute to heightened stress levels, compromised hygiene, and potential health hazards due to the accumulation of dust and bacteria. Furthermore, the maintenance of a tidy and orderly home often reflects one's values regarding responsibility, respect for shared spaces, and attention to detail. Failure to address these issues proactively can lead to escalating tensions and dissatisfaction within the relationship. If a man's standard is a clean home, and he enters into a relationship with a woman whose home is unkempt, the relationship may become as "unkempt" as her living environment is.

"IF A PERSON YIELDS TO A DIFFERENT FAITH FOR THE RELATIONSHIP, IT CAN RAISE QUESTIONS ABOUT WHAT OTHER COMPROMISES THEY HAVE MADE."

CHAPTER 15
DIFFERING BELIEFS

Sometimes, opposites attract, and differences are a good thing. However, when it comes to belief systems, differences may be detrimental to a relationship.

In the early stages of a relationship, differences are often swept under the rug. Tentative compromises may be made or differences may even be ignored entirely to keep the relationship moving smoothly. Yet, ignoring such major differences or making temporary compromises will not suffice in the long run.

When seeking a potential wife, addressing different belief systems head-on is essential. Otherwise, the following problems may get in the way.

DIFFERING RELIGIOUS PRACTICES

Religion is a significant part of most peoples life and most people are unyielding about their faith. For couples with differing religious backgrounds, reconciling their differences can prove to be a daunting task. Each religion has unique practices, rituals, and traditions, which can pose challenges when deciding which ones to adopt in a shared household.

If a person yields to a different faith for the relationship, it can raise questions about what other compromises they have made. Furthermore, religion and culture are closely intertwined, which makes navigating their differences all the more challenging.

This matter becomes even more complicated when children are involved. If Mom and Dad are from two different religious backgrounds, deciding what beliefs and practices to instill in their children will be a challenge. The struggle can become exceptionally challenging during holidays, cultural and religious celebrations. Merging each other's traditions and customs will cause conflicts, and the only way to achieve peace is through compromise.

DIFFERING POLITICAL VIEWS

Religious beliefs aren't the only value system that can get the best of a couple. While some people can set politics aside for the sake of relationships, some feel strongly enough about political ideologies that simply co-existing with someone who doesn't share the same views can be overwhelming. Election seasons tend to be contentious, and when a couple has enormously different beliefs across political party lines, that contention can seep into the household.

Politics is full of sensitive and controversial topics that can often lead to heated debates. From issues related to race, gender equality, abortion, LGBTQ rights, the economy, gun control, foreign policy, and more, it can be challenging to navigate these sensitive issues with someone whose beliefs differ from our own. This can even make it feel like they're living with an enemy, potentially creating a toxic environment that will damage their relationships.

Navigating the complex landscape of politics can be incredibly challenging when children are involved, and parents hold conflicting views. This is particularly true when discussing social issues and teaching children about the nuances and complexities of different perspectives. Even well-intentioned parents can find it problematic to navigate these waters without causing undue stress or conflict within the family.

RELATIVES

Extended families can complicate matters further. Sometimes, relatives may not approve or support a relationship with someone from a different religion and with various political beliefs. If attitudes about religion and politics are extreme, it can be a challenge to balance being respectful while maintaining one's autonomy and ideologies.

Of course, religion and politics aren't the only areas that can cause friction between a man and his partner. Other areas include the following.

DIFFERING PHILOSOPHIES AND SPIRITUALITY

Many women hold philosophical and spiritual beliefs, which can influence their decision-making, goal-setting, and sense of purpose. Some may not adhere to traditional religious or political views. However, if a man's beliefs conflict with a woman's philosophical or spiritual views, it can create ongoing conflict and problems in their relationship.

DIFFERING PERSONAL BELIEFS

Not all belief systems revolve around religion, politics, philosophy, or spirituality. Some beliefs are more personal in origin but still challenge couples if opposing views are held. These personal beliefs may include opinions about wearing revealing clothing, having friends of the opposite sex, and attitudes toward certain ethnic groups and socioeconomic statuses. When a couple's differing beliefs on these matters are deeply connected to lifestyle habits, they can become sources of contention.

CONCLUSION

Differing views, beliefs, and opinions can be captivating, opening doors for deep and enlightening conversations. However, when views, beliefs, and opinions on significant topics are too opposed, they can challenge a couple attempting to merge their lives. Certain matters can't be compromised. For this reason, it is paramount for a man to understand how he differs from his partner in these areas. A marriage that forces these issues under the rug is a marriage that will eventually trip and fall on that rug.

"IT IS ESSENTIAL TO CONSIDER WHETHER ONE'S PARTNER STRUGGLES WITH SELF-CONTROL, ANGER MANAGEMENT, MENTAL STABILITY, OR SUBSTANCE ABUSE, AS THESE FACTORS CAN NEGATIVELY IMPACT A RELATIONSHIP."

CHAPTER 16
POLICE RECORD

On average, the majority of women with police records have been arrested for offenses related to substance abuse, mental illness, or spousal abuse. While a criminal record does not necessarily indicate a person's character or suitability for marriage, it is crucial to be aware of previous encounters with the law, as they can potentially have implications in certain areas.

TRUST AND TRANSPARENCY

Past issues with law enforcement can raise issues regarding trust and transparency, especially if a woman is tight-lipped about the circumstances that led to her arrest. Depending on the offense, there may be traits in her character she wishes to hide or accountability that she is avoiding. It is essential to consider whether one's partner struggles with self-control, anger management, mental stability, or substance abuse, as these factors can negatively impact a relationship.

LEGAL AND FINANCIAL IMPLICATIONS

A police record can have far-reaching consequences, making obtaining specific licenses, employment, or housing difficult. If a police record is holding a woman back in certain areas of her life, it can increase the burden on her partner and be an all-around inconvenience for the family.

RISK OF REPEATED OFFENSES

Depending on the nature of the offense, there can be a risk of a woman repeating the behavior that got her in trouble. This is especially true if her arrest involved drug or substance abuse. Unless a woman has effectively addressed these issues, relapses are likely to occur. If a partner is unprepared for the possibility of relapse, recurring behavior can be incredibly distressing and pose a considerable challenge to maintaining a healthy relationship.

*(Substance use is addressed chapter 24 / page 95)

STIGMA AND SOCIAL PERCEPTION

There's often social stigma connected to having a police record, especially for women. A man dating or married to a woman with a record may find that judgment from family, friends, and the community they live in can be a hassle. If the relationship is not based on a solid foundation, the social stigma will be a source of embarrassment.

EMOTIONAL AND PSYCHOLOGICAL IMPACT

Dealing with the repercussions of a police record can be emotionally and psychologically hard on both partners. A woman with a record may experience shame, guilt, and anxiety regarding her past, and her emotions will affect her partner. A woman may struggle to move forward if she hasn't come to terms with her past.

LEGAL CONCERNS

If children are involved, a woman's police record can impact custody arrangements, especially if she has children from a previous relationship. As discussed earlier, being involved with a woman who has children from a prior relationship is challenging in its own right. If the woman in question has a criminal past and consequently is dealing with a custody issue, the problems all become that much more complicated for a new partner to deal with.

RESTRICTIONS

The aftermath of an arrest may include restrictions and limitations on travel capabilities or financial opportunities, which can be an inconvenience should a romantic partner want to travel or need financial help supporting the household.

CONCLUSION

The past does not always have to define a person. No one is faultless, and everyone makes mistakes. Plenty of people grow to improve their lives for the better. However, when it comes to having a police record, the past can have consequences that make it that much more difficult. In choosing a wife, it is essential to be realistic and calculate if the relationship and your future goals will be troubled by her past conviction.

"A WOMAN WHO TAKES A LACKADAISICAL VIEW OF THIS MATTER MIGHT EXTEND THE SAME CARELESS ATTITUDE TOWARD OTHER DECISIONS IN HER PERSONAL LIFE."

CHAPTER 17
BAD CREDIT

Financial hardship can happen to anyone, often resulting in a poor credit score. However, having a poor credit history doesn't necessarily reflect a person's character or suitability as a partner for marriage. Nonetheless, if you're considering marrying a woman with a bad credit history, there are several aspects to consider.

VALUE

The borrowing and repayment process demonstrates one's reliability and trustworthiness. However, a woman who takes a lackadaisical view of this matter might extend the same careless attitude toward other decisions in her personal life. Traits such as a lack of planning, irresponsibility with budgeting can have a detrimental effect on a family's reputation and financial future.

A woman's creditworthiness, denoting her reliability in repaying borrowed funds, is a valuable indicator of her financial sensibleness, responsibility, and overall integrity. Conversely, a bad credit history may suggest the contrary, potentially precipitating financial adversities that create stress and challenges, ultimately affecting a family's well-being.

CREDIT SCORE

A woman's poor credit score can significantly affect her spouse's credit, particularly in joint financial endeavors such as buying a home or establishing shared bank accounts. When one partner's financial mismanagement affects the other, it can create embarrassment and obstacles to building a stable family life. Such challenges will hinder a man's ability to provide for the family's needs effectively.

DEBT ACCUMULATION

If the woman you are pursuing for marriage has poor credit, she has more than likely accumulated debt, which could create issues even after the Marriage. Her debt will become a shared responsibility with her husband, which means that any debt she has accumulated in the past will could be a joint liability and potentially limit the family's financial freedom.

FINANCIAL STRAIN

Money management is essential in marriages, and complications can prevent a couple from living comfortably and planning for the future.

In a marriage, a woman's financial mismanagement can lead to a pervasive sense of mistrust in the relationship. This effect can be compounded by the perception that a partner is unable to competently manage finances, which may lead to feelings of dis-empowerment and resentment. The outcome of this dynamic is an unhealthy and unsustainable balance between the two.

A woman's money mismanagement can significantly impact her husband's bank account, creating financial strain and discord within the relationship. Whether it stems from overspending, accumulating debt, or failing to budget effectively, poor financial habits can lead to shared financial repercussions. In a partnership where finances are intertwined, one partner's financial decisions inevitably affect the household's overall financial health. The strain of covering unexpected expenses or shouldering a disproportionate share of financial responsibilities can breed resentment and erode trust between spouses.

FINANCIAL OPPORTUNITIES

Bad credit can limit a couple's ability to secure loans, mortgages, and lines of credit. Significant milestones and goals like purchasing a house and starting a family can become such overwhelming burdens that they feel impossible when limited in these areas. Being unable to achieve goals and make plans due to financial limitations will limit a man from providing for the future for his family.

QUALITY OF LIFESTYLE

Dealing with financial strain, debt, and poor credit will limit a couple's access to specific amenities, travel for leisure, and participation in recreational hobbies. Relationships need fun and opportunities to alleviate stress. Still, these things can be hard to come by when money is always a concern, which leads to resentment, particularly for the partner who "inherited" the other's financial struggles.

FUTURE PLANNING

When a significant amount of time, energy, and resources are spent on dealing with debt and repairing bad credit, there may be little left to save for retirement, college education for children, or long-term investments. The inability to plan for the future can make it appear daunting and uncertain.

EMOTIONAL TOLL

Money struggles often lead to anxiety and depression, causing a couple to fear never recovering.

- The partner who caused the bulk of the financial strain may be plagued with guilt. Additionally, a fear of abandonment may be persistent. Consequently, this person may feel compelled to hold on to the relationship at all costs, fearing being unable to survive alone.

- On the other hand, the partner who bears the burden of the other may feel resentful and consider being better off alone or with someone more financially responsible.

CONCLUSION

Marriage is a union based on love, but it's essential to acknowledge the role of finances in the relationship and how it is managed. Before choosing a potential spouse, it's vital to have open and honest discussions about each other's financial standing, including credit and indebtedness. Failure to do so often creates tension in the marriage, especially if you're not prepared to take on more debt than you had before entering the relationship.

"BENEATH THE SURFACE LIES A CALCULATED AGENDA TO FULFILL THEIR SELFISH DESIRES, DEVOID OF ANY GENUINE EMOTIONAL CONNECTION OR EMPATHY."

CHAPTER 18
NARCISSISTIC BEHAVIOR

If you are in a relationship with a narcissist, my condolences. If you haven't tied the knot, please heed this chapter.

Being romantically involved with a woman who possesses narcissistic traits or worse, full-blown narcissistic personality disorder, will be one of the most toxic relationships you can ever experience. Narcissistic personality disorder (NPD) is a condition in which an individual has a grossly inflated sense of self-importance, an obsessive need for admiration, and a lack of empathy for others.

The struggles of being in a relationship with a narcissist can cover an entire book alone. However, this chapter will briefly present some of the "Red Flags" to look for.

LOVE BOMBING

A narcissist, driven by their insatiable need for admiration and validation, often resorts to a manipulative tactic known as love bombing to ensnare a partner. At the outset of the relationship, they shower their partner with excessive compliments, grand gestures of affection, and lots of sexual attention. This intense and overwhelming barrage of attention creates an illusion of a perfect romance, captivating their mate and clouding their judgment. The narcissist strategically crafts a facade of adoration and devotion, exploiting their partner's vulnerabilities and insecurities to establish control and dominance. However, beneath the surface lies a calculated agenda to fulfill their selfish desires, devoid of any genuine emotional connection or empathy. As the relationship progresses, the love bombing fades, revealing the narcissist's true colors and leaving their mate disillusioned and emotionally depleted.

Love bombing can be confusing for the recipient. It places the victim under the narcissist's control, for love bombing is usually mistaken for actual love. The recipient might incorrectly assume the narcissist is the best lover he has ever had. But unfortunately, it is all an act, a phase in a toxic, cyclical pattern. Why? Because narcissists are mentally incapable of establishing emotional connections with others. Their primary objective is to enforce control over others for their benefit.

LACK OF EMPATHY

Narcissism is also characterized by a lack of empathy, meaning that narcissistic women are unable to comprehend the emotions and perspectives of others. This can cause their partners to feel emotionally disconnected and misunderstood, leading to an unbalanced relationship.

A narcissist usually displays feigned empathy and sympathy for self-serving ulterior motives. This is done as a means to cling to the relationship for her selfish needs.

MANIPULATIVE BEHAVIOR

Manipulation is a favorite practice of narcissists, helping them maintain control of romantic partners and relationships. Lying, gas-lighting, and exploitation are all tools a narcissist will use to keep the upper hand over their partners and others.

DIFFICULTY RESOLVING CONFLICT

A woman with Narcissistic Personality Disorder (NPD) will find it difficult to resolve conflicts because she will never admit to being at fault. She sees herself as faultless and avoids taking responsibility or being accountable for her actions whenever there are problems. Rather than acknowledging her mistakes, apologizing, or working towards finding solutions, she blames others. This makes it unlikely that any conflicts will be resolved effectively in a marriage. The partner of a narcissist will usually have to compromise or evade most conflictual situations.

COMMUNICATION STRUGGLES

Narcissists love attention and have an unhealthy appetite to make sure they are at the center of it. For this reason, communicating and holding meaningful conversations with a narcissistic can be a challenge.

She will dominate conversations and dismiss your thoughts and ideas, that is, when not stealing and taking credit for them. When in a relationship, the partner of a narcissist will be made to feel unimportant and will often find that expressing one's self is a fruitless endeavor.

SENSE OF ENTITLEMENT

Because narcissists have inflated egos and an exaggerated sense of self-importance, they expect others to treat them as they see themselves, which means a narcissist will typically feel entitled to special treatment. This attitude can be draining to a romantic partner. Resentment will arise in the relationship for two reasons.

- The narcissist will do her best to convince a partner that she isn't being appreciated enough.

- The partner will feel unappreciated in comparison.

THE CONSTANT NEED FOR VALIDATION

Right on the heels of needing constant attention is needing constant validation. Narcissists think highly of themselves and feed off the validation that being important and admired provides them. This can place a partner under pressure to dish out praise to avoid conflict constantly. Over time, this will become exhausting.

ISOLATION

Narcissists have a strong desire for control, especially when it comes to their romantic partners. This is why they often resort to isolating their partners from family and friends. They do not tolerate outside interference and strive to ensure that their romantic partner's attention is solely focused on them. The need to be the center of the universe usually compels a narcissist to take calculated steps to push everyone close to their partner away.

- A narcissistic person often isolates her partner from their social circle and increase their own sense of importance.

HIGH EXPECTATIONS

Narcissists may set impossibly high expectations on their partners because they crave a partner who makes them look good. Due to the narcissist's limited emotional capacity, the relationship may not be based on love; instead, it may be more about appearance. Consequently, narcissist usually have unrealistic expectations from their partner, and when those expectations are not met, they tend to move in the discard phase of the relationship.

Unmet goals and expectations are often the catalyst of the abuse suffered at the hands of a narcissist. The issue can trigger emotional roller-coaster highs and lows. The abuse is often emotional and verbal, which can be enormously detrimental to the partner's self-esteem.

ABUSE

Victims of narcissistic abuse are often left with deep emotional wounds that can be difficult to heal alone. A narcissist's manipulation and abuse may erode their victim's sense of self-worth, leaving behind lasting scars. Constant gas-lighting and invalidation can lead to feelings of worthlessness, confusion, and self-doubt. Survivors of narcissistic abuse often need counseling and a supportive environment to process their trauma, regain their sense of identity, and rebuild their self-esteem.

CONCLUSION

Without counseling, a narcissist is likely to continue their manipulative behaviors unabated, perpetuating a cycle of control and emotional harm. Lacking insight into their own actions and unwilling to acknowledge the impact of their behavior on others, they persist in seeking validation and admiration at the expense of their victims' well-being. Without intervention, the narcissist's toxic patterns will persist, perpetuating a cycle of abuse that can have devastating consequences for their victims' mental and emotional health.

These issues only scratch the surface of what marriage to a narcissist can be like. So if a woman shows any of these "Red Flags", it's best to turn away while you can. Beneath the surface lies a calculated agenda to fulfill their selfish desires, devoid of any genuine emotional connection or empathy.

"THE NARCISSIST STRATEGICALLY CRAFTS A FACADE OF ADORATION AND DEVOTION, EXPLOITING THEIR PARTNER'S VULNERABILITIES AND INSECURITIES TO ESTABLISH CONTROL AND DOMINANCE."

A. LAMAR

"A MAN SHOULD NEVER HAVE TO COMPETE FOR HIS WOMAN, HIS CHILDREN OR HIS POSITION AS HEAD OF THE HOUSE."

CHAPTER 19
DOESN'T RESPECT HEADSHIP

In traditional households, it is customary for men to assume the role of the head of the household and take on leadership of his family. It is important to note, however, that this does not entail behaving like a dictator and dominating every aspect of a family. Instead, men have a significant responsibility to ensure that their homes are safe, provided for, and full of love.

Respect plays a vital role in enabling a man to provide and lead his household effectively. The challenge arises when his position as the head of the family is contested. In such situations, having a partner who challenges his role is perceived as a sign of disrespect, which can lead to significant problems in the relationship.

Here is a list of what could happen when a woman has no respect for the head of her household.

POWER AND RESPECT

When both spouses are vying for the position of head of household, the power dynamic of the relationship will struggle. Rather than leading the household, much time and energy will be spent on each partner trying to gain the upper hand. A man should never have to compete for his woman, his children, or his position as head of the house. When a man is providing for the household, having a wife as a compliment to help and support their home is a plus. A marriage in this way will allow the household to thrive.

APPRECIATION

When each spouse is appreciated for their respective roles, it naturally breeds respect. It will be hard to maintain mutual respect when a woman does not acknowledge her spouse's role and challenges him for it. A man will not do well feeling undermined in his household, and a woman will struggle to maintain the respect of a man who views her as dismissive of his instinct to lead, protect and provide for the family. Relationships cannot survive without mutual respect.

A woman who is hesitant to relinquish leadership in the household may exhibit indications of control-related issues and a propensity for dominance within the relationship. Consequently, she is likely to experience frequent conflicts with a strong, authoritative partner who demonstrates leadership qualities and a natural inclination for providing.

Constantly being disregarded as the head of the household and dealing with a woman who aims to dominate can cause a man's self-esteem to take a hit over time. Feelings of invalidation and unimportance can potentially destroy his confidence, effectively creating a man who does not want to lead and provide for his household. He'll just simply give up or look for a different circumstance where he feels appreciated.

COMMUNICATION BREAKDOWNS

Effective communication is absolutely essential in a healthy relationship. However, if a wife fails to demonstrate respect for her husband's role as the head of the household, it usually results in a severe communication breakdown. This leads to a man feeling disrespected and voiceless, causing significant difficulties in decision-making, conflict resolution, and reaching mutually beneficial compromises.

RESENTMENT

When communications break down, and a man cannot fulfill the role that comes naturally to him, he will ultimately resent his partner. This will make the relationship feel unworthy of continuing, leading to unbearable animosity between the two partners. Often some men under this condition won't continue loving and wholeheartedly providing for a partner they resent, for the animosity will become unbearable.

THE FAMILY

By disregarding the traditional roles and dynamics of marriage, she may undermine her husband's authority and create tension and conflict. This can erode trust and respect between them, potentially causing emotional strain and marital discord. Additionally, her actions may confuse children or other family members about the structure of authority within the household, leading to further disruption.

CONCLUSION

A marriage can be successful if each person understands their duties and responsibilities and has a mutually agreed-upon arrangement for sharing and dividing those responsibilities.

The roles of husband and wife come with traditionally defined tasks and contributions, equally important to a household's success. If a woman has control issues that cause her to desire the role typically reserved for her husband, the household unity will suffer. It undermines the foundational principles of mutual respect, communication, and partnership essential for a healthy relationship. This lack of respect may make a man feel emasculated and frustrated, eroding trust and intimacy. Moreover, it can create an imbalance of power dynamics, fostering resentment and discord. If a woman doesn't respect her boundaries and come to terms with your rightful position within the partnership, it's a clear sign that this relationship is headed for a disrespectful end.

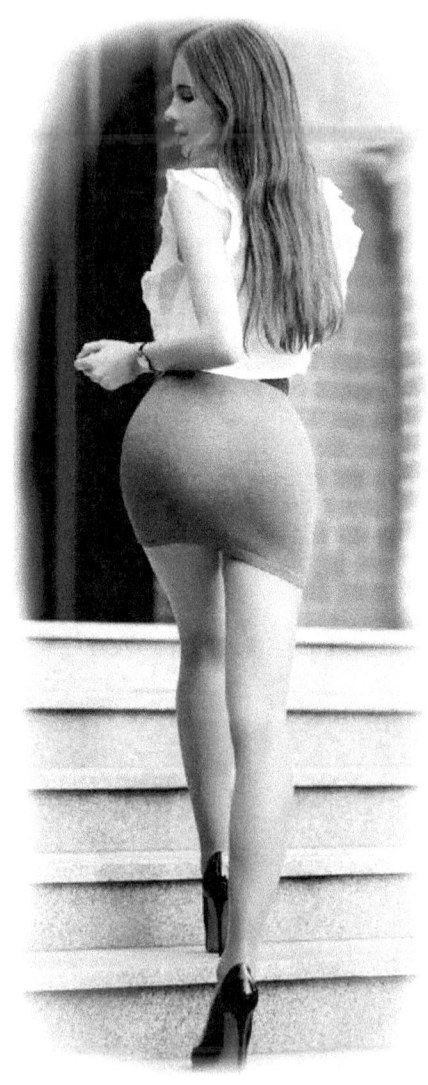

"IF SHE LIKES ATTENTION FROM OTHER MEN, THERE MAY COME A TIME WHEN SHE WANTS MORE THAN JUST ATTENTION."

CHAPTER 20
LIKES MALE ATTENTION

It is normal to appreciate and enjoy attention from others. However, a fine line exists between normal and being needy for attention.

A woman who constantly seeks attention from men, including those she is not romantically involved with, may be internally battling a deeper psychological or emotional issue. A need for attention may indicate her feelings of insecurity and low self-esteem, consequently seeking attention as validation. For women with these emotional issues, attention can become addictive, and they may be unwilling or unable to give it up, even when in a serious relationship. This is simply a breeding ground for complications in the relationship.

Here are the problems a man may encounter when his partner is obsessed with attention from other men.

VALIDATION

Some women that feel overlooked or unappreciated turn to dressing in provocative clothing. Seeking external validation through attention from other men might provide a temporary sense of empowerment or worthiness.

In addition to emotional issues, society as a whole and pressures related to beauty and sexuality can impact a woman's perception of herself and her self-worth. This may lead her to believe dressing provocatively is necessary to feel attractive and desirable. This behavior may escalate into other Undesirable traits, such as flirting and communicating with other men to fulfill her perceived needs that are not being met in her current relationship.

JEALOUSY, INSECURITY, AND MISTRUST

Often, attention-seeking behavior involves some level of secrecy or deception. This can create a climate of distrust within the marriage, leading the spouse to question his wife's honesty and intentions.

Even if the woman has no intention of leaving her relationship, the act of seeking attention elsewhere can make a man feel inadequate. He might compare himself to the other man, leading to feelings of insecurity and a loss of self-esteem.

Depending on the level of attention-seeking behavior, the woman might unintentionally (or intentionally) cross emotional boundaries with the other man. This can be incredibly damaging to the relationship, creating a deep sense of betrayal and insecurity in a significant other.

SELF-SABOTAGING BEHAVIORS

Low self-esteem can lead to a cycle of self-sabotage. A woman might unconsciously create situations where she craves external attention, even if it puts her relationship at risk. This could be a way to reinforce negative beliefs about herself or her relationship.

DIFFICULTY COMMUNICATING NEEDS

Some women, especially those raised in emotionally closed environments, may struggle to express their emotional needs directly to their significant other. Seeking attention outside the relationship, even unintentionally, could be a distorted attempt to communicate a desire for more connection or validation within the relationship.

PAST FAILED RELATIONSHIPS

Negative experiences in past relationships can create lasting insecurities. Attention from another man can be a temporary fix for those feelings, offering a sense of security and desirability that may be missing in her current marriage.

Past experiences with failed relationships, especially those marked by rejection or lack of validation, can leave a woman questioning her self-worth. Attention from another man, even if fleeting, can act as a temporary balm for those emotional wounds and provide a sense of validation.

KEEPS OTHER MALE COMPANY

A woman who has a man but often keeps the company of other males might be doing so for questionable reasons. It could indicate a lack of satisfaction or fulfillment in her primary relationship, leading her to seek attention and validation elsewhere. This behavior can also suggest a disregard for her partner's feelings, potentially causing mistrust and insecurity. It may also indicate that she enjoys the thrill of flirting or the sense of power that comes from having multiple men interested in her. By having close associations with other men, she might be prioritizing their company over her commitment to her relationship, which could be seen as disrespectful to her partner and indicative of deeper issues within the relationship.

CONCLUSION

At stated, some men like their women to dress sexy and don't mind the attention it brings her. But if a man is of the other sort regarding a woman's attention-seeking behavior from others, it will create a heightened sense of stress and anxiety in the relationship. It will also challenge a man's respect, and historically, serious conflicts and fights have been the end result. For this reason, if your woman regularly thrives on attention from others, it is of the utmost importance to understand why, and if this causes you internal conflict, it's better for your attention to be turned elsewhere. Why? A man should never tolerate any behavior undermining his dignity, respect, or personal well-being.

"IF A WOMAN'S CAREER COMPLETELY OVERSHADOWS HER SPOUSE AND HOME, FEELINGS OF NEGLECT, FRUSTRATION, AND RESENTMENT ARE BOUND TO STRIKE."

CHAPTER 21
TOO CAREER ORIENTED

Ambition and drive are admirable qualities, and as discussed previously, it can be a "Red Flag" when a woman is content with a low-paying job or not working at all. However, it is essential to have a healthy balance. A woman excessively dedicated to her career is unlikely to maintain that healthy balance and may neglect other aspects of her life such as her marriage, children and household responsibilities.

If a woman's career completely overshadows her spouse and home, feelings of neglect, frustration, and resentment are bound to occur. Especially if she fails to nurture her relationship and perhaps her family life. A woman's role in her home is essential. If she cannot sufficiently juggle the demands of work and home, and is prone to prioritizing work over home, it will inevitably lead to an unhappy household.

Let's take a closer look at the issues that may arise.

IMBALANCED PRIORITIES

When a woman prioritizes work over her family, it can create significant challenges within the home dynamic. The imbalance between professional and familial commitments may lead to feelings of neglect and frustration among family members, particularly if they rely on her for emotional support, care, and attention.

This lead to:

- A decrease in emotional connection, for there will be little opportunity outside of her work for quality time and conversation.

- A decrease in physical intimacy, for her energy may often be depleted by the time she finished her work day.

- When a woman consistently prioritizes her work schedule over her spouse, it can lead to the erosion of trust and communication, as the spouse may feel neglected and uncertain about their place in her priorities.

CHILDREN

When there are children in the home, they will feel this same neglect. Between her work hours and their school hours, she may have little time to interact with her children, which leads to:

- Missing out on significant milestones made by the children.

- Missing out on family time and activities.

- A lack of emotional connection to and from the children.

- Children who feel their mom loves her job more than she loves them, potentially resulting in long-term emotional and psychological damage.

- Children may grow up to follow their mother's example, prioritizing work over maintaining healthy and meaningful relationships.

- A spouse who feels that he is essentially parenting alone often grow resentful about whom he selected as a life partner.

BURN-OUT

A woman who finds it difficult to establish a healthy balance between her work and personal life may struggle with issues related to selfishness, time management, or both. This may result in her inability to disconnect from work even when she is not on the job and not being fully present in other areas of her life. Not only will this impact her relationships with her spouse and children, but she may also experience stress and burnout as a result.

FAILED CONFLICT-RESOLUTION

It will be difficult for a man to resolve conflict with a significant other who is regularly too busy with career commitments. If her time, focus, and energy are always spent on work, getting her to pay attention to issues outside of work, let alone resolving them will be challenging. This kind of breakdown in communication will be highly detrimental to the relationship, and conflicts may be neglected for so long that they cease to have a solution.

CONCLUSION

While a woman's dedication and commitment to her career can be impressive, if she prioritizes it over her family, such dedication and commitment will backfire. If she does not establish a healthy work-life balance, it will ultimately cause friction in the family, and she may wind up with a family that feels disconnected from her.

When selecting a wife, there is nothing wrong with choosing a woman who finds her career fulfilling. However, ensure she understands that a career is replaceable, but the time with her family is not.

"SOME WOMEN WHO GREW UP AS THE ONLY CHILD MAY FEEL NEGLECTED IF HER PARTNER DOES NOT MAKE HER THE CENTER OF HIS UNIVERSE."

CHAPTER 22
AN ONLY CHILD

Siblings are our first friends and provide us with our first experiences in learning to get along with others. Birth order tends to play a hug role in personality development, with distinct personality traits associated with the eldest child, the middle children, and the youngest child. Distinct traits are associated with being the only child as well.

In comparison to children with siblings, an only child typically grows up accustomed to high levels of attention. They also grow up learning to be self-reliant and independent, not regularly sharing space and needing to compromise with others during their most formative years. These traits may serve them well in some areas of life, but they can pose a challenge in terms of managing romantic relationships.

Here are some of the components potentially involved with entering a relationship with a woman who is an only child.

HIGH EXPECTATIONS FOR ATTENTION

Due to having her parents' undivided attention during childhood, an only child may expect such devotion and undivided attention in adult relationships.

Some women who grew up as the only child may feel neglected if her partner does not make her the center of his universe. She may feel her needs are not being validated, which often leads to conflict between the pair.

A romantic partner, particularly one who grew up with siblings, may find this expectation excessive, unusual, or unnatural. His partner's perceived neediness may become a turn-off over time.

If a man with siblings marries an only child, he may notice his spouse's struggle to understand the dynamics of his sibling relationships. If he is close with his siblings, this can be especially problematic, for his spouse may have misplaced jealousy over the attention he gives to his sibling and other family members.

With no siblings of her own, a woman may struggle to connect with brothers and sisters-in-law. If a man's family of origin is important to him, his spouse's lack of understanding and emotional detachment may become a source of contention.

DIFFICULTY SHARING AND COMPROMISING

Lacking experience sharing space, belongings, and resources with siblings may cause an only child to struggle with sharing later in life, including within a marriage. After spending her formative years with some degree of solitude, suddenly having another person to share and compromise with may be disorienting. Conflicts regarding ownership, personal space, and boundaries may result.

Due to the independent and self-reliant nature an only children may develop, merging lives with another person may feel uncomfortable. Marriages require compromise, collaboration, and consideration of the other person's feelings, all of which may be second-nature to a person who grew up with siblings, but foreign to a person who was the only child.

INEXPERIENCE WITH CONFLICT RESOLUTION

Interacting with siblings is often a child's initial experience with friendship and introduces them to their first experiences with conflict as well. This is essential for their character development as sibling disputes help them learn how to manage and resolve differences and disagreements. However, for an only child, the development of these skills may be delayed, which could hinder their ability to resolve conflicts in future adult relationships.

When women who were an only child, have more than one child of her own, the relationships between her children may be foreign to her as well. Her lack of experience with sibling dynamics may hinder her in helping the children develop healthy relationships with each other. Furthermore, when disputes occur amongst her children, her struggles with conflict resolution in her own life will make her inefficient in helping her children resolve issue with each other.

When an only child becomes the mother of multiple children, an overbearing parenting style may form. Inexperience with typical sibling interactions (i.e., playing, rough-housing, arguing, etc.) may be a source of annoyance, resulting in an overcritical mother who does not allow her children to interact in ways that come naturally to them. This behavior may lead to unnecessary resentment or competition between her children.

CONCLUSION

Of course, these issues are not going to be prevalent with every woman who is an only child. Some only children always wanted siblings and happily welcome marrying into a family with siblings and big extended families. Others may have formed sibling-like relationships with friends or cousins, making them familiar with sibling-life despite lacking brothers and/or sisters of their own.

Nevertheless, many women raised as only children grow accustomed to being the sole recipient of attention, thereby never having to share this attention with anyone else. When such traits become ingrained, the adjustments necessary for marriage may pose a challenge that an only child is ill-equipped to handle.

"RESEARCH HAS SHOWN THAT YOUNG PEOPLE IN THEIR EARLY TWENTIES MAY BE MORE IMPULSIVE AND PRONE TO SEEKING NOVELTY AND EXCITEMENT, WHICH CAN CONTRIBUTE TO A TENDENCY TO MOVE IN AND OUT OF RELATIONSHIPS FREQUENTLY."

CHAPTER 23
UNDER THE AGE OF 26

Neuroscience suggests that the human brain does not reach full maturity until the age of 25. Some psychologists even go as far as to call the ages 18 to 24 "late adolescence" rather than young adulthood, acknowledging that the brain, as well as personality and reasoning capabilities, are still developing until the mid-twenties.

Given the magnitude of the commitment that marriage represents, it is often suggested that it is not practical to marry during a time when growth and development are still occurring. Furthermore, taking on the role of spouse, and possibly that of a parent, may preclude pursuing specific opportunities better suited to one's younger years, such as furthering one's education, advancing in one's career, and embarking on journeys of self-discovery. Here are some of the main reasons marriage before the age of 26 may not be the best idea.

LIMITED LIFE EXPERIENCE

Keeping in mind that fully maturing happens later in the twenties and early thirties, a person's life experience, particularly adult life experience, is going to be limited under the age of 26. Marriage requires sufficient experience with compromising, communicating, empathy, problem-solving, money management, and so much more. In short, a person needs to have enough adult years under their belt before successfully merging lives with another adult. At the age of 26, you've literally had one year of being adult with full reasoning capabilities. It is important to be familiar with adulthood before adding on challenging roles like spouse and parent.

RISK OF DIVORCE

Marrying too young is linked to a higher risk of divorce. Younger people are more likely to make impulsive decisions due to limited reasoning abilities, emotional immaturity, and lack of life experience. Someone in their late teens or early twenties may overestimate their readiness for marriage. Only later, after maturing more, may they come to realize a marriage at such a young age was a mistake.

- The late teens and early twenties are a time of identity-formation. People in this age bracket are typically learning and exploring their principles, values, goals, likes and dislikes, and ambitions. Shifts in beliefs and attitudes are not uncommon. Hence, after marrying too young, a person may grow to find that who they have become is no longer compatible with who they were when the marriage occurred.

SOCIAL PRESSURE

Younger people are more easily influenced by societal pressures. Often, young people have not fully learned to think for themselves and to do what is best for them. For example, many women are still targeted with the message that marriage and children should happen under the age of 30. A young woman who takes this message to heart may jump into marriage and motherhood when she isn't truly ready, be it physically, emotionally, or psychologically. This, in turn, may lead her to resent her life choices later. Only with age do people learn the importance of moving through life on a schedule that actually works for them and their partner.

FREEDOM TO ROME

During this youthful stage of life, young women are typically exploring their identities, asserting their independence, and seeking new experiences. Socializing and engaging in recreational activities, such as partying, allows them to connect with peers, establish social bonds, and assert their autonomy.

Young women may be more impulsive and sensation-seeking due to the continued development of the brain's pre-frontal cortex, which is responsible for decision-making and impulse control. *Neuroscience research has shown that young people in their early twenties are often more impulsive and prone to seek novelty and excitement, which can contribute to a tendency to move in and out of relationships frequently.

*HTTPS://WWW.NCBI.NLM.NIH.GOV/PMC/ARTICLES/PMC3621648/

CONCLUSION

Taking on the roles of spouse and parent before simply living enough adult years to get a full understanding of one's self and reach developmental milestones like earning degrees and establishing a career, can have devastating effects later in life. Youth is best lived by the young. When youth is given up too soon in favor of marriage and parenthood, the time can never be taken back.

When a man is selecting a wife, it is integral to make sure that both parties have lived enough life to be up for the challenge of marriage. This is something that is rarely achievable under the age of 26. Marriage is a lifelong commitment, and entering such a commitment before having enough life experience is a sure way to add additional challenges that the marriage may not survive.

"THE SOBER PARTNER CAN FIND THEMSELVES SLIPPING INTO THE SAME PATTERNS OF USE AS THEIR PARTNER, ULTIMATELY COMPROMISING THEIR SOBRIETY AND WELL-BEING."

CHAPTER 24
DRINKING AND DRUGS

"It's just marijuana and I only drink on the weekends." If a man is serious about his future with a woman who indulges in drugs or alcohol frequently and brushes it off as an innocent activity, his future may be going up in smoke.

Here are just some of the areas that will be affected by a partner's drinking and drug usage.

THE ABUSE CYCLE

As time passes, it's common for what started as one or two drinks or a simple weekend puff to graduate into a habitual pattern of daily use. Its noteworthy that a majority of individuals who abuse drugs began this journey with casual drinking or being passed a joint for the first time. These seemingly innocent and trivial activities frequently pave the way for drug and alcohol abuse, which can have far more serious consequences than just a temporary buzz.

When a sober partner enters a relationship with someone who frequently uses drugs or drinks regularly, they might initially believe they can maintain their sobriety while condoning their partner's lifestyle. However, over time, the constant exposure to substance use can erode their resolve and trigger cravings or feelings of missing out.

One might start rationalizing occasional use to bond with their partner or alleviate discomfort in social situations. Slowly, their boundaries blur, and what was once a firm stance against substance use becomes more flexible. The sober partner can find themselves slipping into the same patterns of use as their partner, ultimately compromising their sobriety and well-being.

IMPAIRED JUDGMENT

Marrying someone who frequents mind altering substances poses significant challenges in a relationship, including financial strain, trust issues, legal consequences, erratic behavior, mood swings, and impaired decision-making. Families with substance use problems are more likely to have domestic violence and emotional abuse, putting both the spouse and any children's emotional and physical safety at risk.

INFIDELITY

A woman who regularly consumes drugs and alcohol may be at a heightened risk of infidelity due to the impairments these substances can cause in judgment, inhibition, and decision-making. Substance use can lower inhibitions and impair cognitive functions, potentially leading to a lack of regard for consequences and an increased willingness to engage in risky behaviors, including infidelity.

Additionally, substance use may contribute to relationship conflicts, emotional instability, and a diminished sense of commitment, further increasing the likelihood of seeking extramarital affairs or casual encounters. The altered state of mind induced by drugs and alcohol may also distort perceptions of intimacy and loyalty, making it easier to justify infidelity or seek emotional validation outside the primary relationship. Thus, a woman who uses drugs and alcohol faces a heightened risk of infidelity, which can strain relationships and lead to profound emotional consequences for both herself and her partner.

HEALTH CONCERNS

Excessive alcohol and drug usage is bad for your health. The risks can be both physical and mentally impairing and sometimes fatal. No man will be comfortable watching his partner deteriorate from her addiction, potentially putting herself at risk with alcoholism or drug overdose. Alcohol and drugs including those prescribed that get abused, can lead to long-term health battles, all of which will drastically diminish a couple's quality of life together.

FINANCIAL STRAIN

A woman who frequently uses alcohol or drugs often uses the household finances to support her habit or may resort to other dubious means to

acquire it if she is hiding the abuse. Addiction is expensive, and people with an addiction will often prioritize money for their personal use, ignoring more important and necessary expenses.

Legally speaking, the consequences of alcoholism and drug usage can be expensive as well. Being charged with drug possession or DUI can present additional expenses and stress that ultimately hurt the household finances.

Alcohol and drug usage will impair a person's ability to work and maintain a job, which significantly affects the household income.

If alcohol and drug-related health problems develop, medical bills and expenses may pile up.

FAMILY

Frequent use of these substances often results in the user being ostracized by their family. Family members and friends may keep their distance, creating a sense of isolation for the married couple. The spouse may find himself having to cope with his wife's addiction alone, without the help and support of loved ones.

The judgment and isolation stemming from family and friends may become a source of embarrassment. Alcoholics and drug users often try to hide their addictions for this very reason. Often, due to the embarrassment, many men help hide the issue themselves, making it all the more difficult to seek the needed help.

IMPACT ON CHILDREN

Substance abuse during pregnancy can lead to a range of serious health complications for the baby, including low birth weight, premature birth, birth defects, and developmental delays. Additionally, infants born to mothers who use drugs or alcohol during pregnancy may experience neonatal abstinence syndrome (NAS), a condition characterized by withdrawal symptoms such as tremors, seizures, and respiratory distress.

The long-term effects of prenatal exposure to drugs and alcohol can have lasting implications on the child's physical, cognitive, and emotional development.

A mother may neglect her children while under the influence and potentially place them in danger due to her lack of awareness while under the influence.

A mother's addiction can even put the children at risk of being removed from the household by child protective services. The children of people with an addiction often end up in foster care, dealing with the instability of being moved from one residence to another.

Witnessing their mother's usage poses a risk for the children growing up to develop the same habits and addiction. Children of alcoholics and addicts often develop severe behavioral and emotional issues that follow them into adulthood.

DOMESTIC VIOLENCE

Research in psychology consistently indicates that individuals under the influence of alcohol or drugs frequently exhibit heightened aggression and are more prone to engaging in violent behavior Yes, even women. When violence occurs, it's usually directed at the people closest to them, her spouse and children. Physical, mental, and emotional abuse can all become prevalent, leading to long-lasting trauma in those victimized by an abusive wife and mother.

CONCLUSION

A man must confront the harsh reality of what might be driving his partner to escape through mind-altering substances or heavy drinking, even if occasionally. If he seeks a long-term relationship with a woman who frequently indulges in these behaviors and is unwilling to change, he must put his future well-being and stability above all else. Ignoring these "Red Flags" and pursuing this relationship could lead to severe emotional and psychological damage, jeopardizing his personal and professional life. Being brutally honest and prioritizing his safety and stability over potential romantic illusions is crucial.

"THE MAJORITY OF INDIVIDUALS WHO ABUSE DRUGS BEGAN THIS JOURNEY WITH CASUAL DRINKING OR BEING PASSED A JOINT FOR THE FIRST TIME."

"WOMEN WHO EXHIBIT SUCH BEHAVIOR LIKELY USE THEIR LOOKS TO SATISFY THEIR NEED FOR ADMIRATION."

CHAPTER 25
OBSESSED WITH APPEARANCE

A woman who takes care of her appearance and presents herself attractively is admirable. However, it's essential to exercise a balance between self-care and an unhealthy obsession with one's looks, which can have adverse effects on both physical and mental health.

When a man is seeking a life partner, it is important to observe whether the attention the woman gives to her appearance is simply a sign of her caring about how she presents herself, or if there may be deeper underlying issues at play.

NARCISSISTIC TRAITS

Focusing too much on one's appearance can be a sign of narcissism. If a woman is excessively preoccupied with her physical appearance to the extent that it gives her an inflated sense of self-importance, it could indicate that she has a grandiose personality. Women who exhibit such behavior likely use their looks to satisfy their need for admiration. This excessive need for attention can have a negative impact on the relationship, making the woman appear shallow and prioritizing superficiality over building deeper emotional connections.

LOW SELF-ESTEEM

A woman who places significant emphasis on her outward appearance may indicate low self-esteem and feelings of inadequacy in other aspects of her life. This preoccupation with superficial attributes and the opinions of others may suggest that she uses her appearance as a metric for determining her self-worth. It is important to note that various factors beyond her control, such as age, health, accidents, and illness, will ultimately have an impact on her physical appearance. Consequently, a woman whose self-worth is linked to her appearance may experience emotional turmoil when her looks no longer conform to her desired standards.

BODY DYSMORPHIA

It's common for women to be concern with their appearance, but this may not necessarily be due to a desire to be beautiful. Rather, it could be driven by a fear of being unattractive. Body dysmorphic disorder is a mental condition in which an individual is overly concerned about their physical appearance, often perceiving flaws or inadequacies that are not noticeable to others.

This can lead to an obsessive fixation on "fixing" these perceived flaws, with the goal of achieving an unrealistic standard of perfection that is unattainable. Consequently, some individuals may resort to extreme measures such as unnecessary cosmetic surgeries or body part enhancements, which is expensive and can endanger their health, all in the pursuit of trying to achieve a level of physical perfection.

CONCLUSION

It's natural for women to want to present themselves in the best possible way. As stated earlier, an obsession often reflects deep-seated insecurities or a desire for external validation, which can lead to constant self-scrutiny, excessive spending on beauty products and procedures, and prioritizing superficial looks over meaningful connection and emotional intimacy. This fixation can cause emotional neglect, as the emphasis on appearance may overshadow the development of deeper bonds and mutual support.

Additionally, this often leads to unhealthy behaviors, such as disordered eating or compulsive exercise, further straining a relationship. Over time, the relentless pursuit of physical perfection can create a superficial and unstable foundation for any marriage, undermining trust, communication, and long-term happiness. While physical attractiveness is undoubtedly appealing to most, it's important to note that if a woman's physical appearance is the only admirable trait she possesses, the relationship will be superficial and lacking in any real depth and as shallow as her looks.

"THIS PREOCCUPATION WITH SUPERFICIAL ATTRIBUTES AND THE OPINIONS OF OTHERS MAY SUGGEST THAT SHE USES HER APPEARANCE AS A METRIC FOR DETERMINING HER SELF-WORTH."

"SELECTING THE RIGHT WOMAN FOR THIS PARTNERSHIP IS THE MOST IMPORTANT DECISION YOU WILL EVER MAKE."

Chapter 26
SUMMARY

Marriage is one of the most important decisions a man will make in his life. Selecting a wife is a life-altering decision, and when embarking on such a decision, one should hope it is for the better, not the worse. So how does one make the right choice?

As an example, let's compare marriage to a business transaction:

A wise businessman seeking a partner to expand his business would first understand his own value. He would conduct thorough research to identify a partner who shares his values and goals and assess their reputation, financial stability, compatibility, leadership qualities, and communication style. He'll also note whether previous partners hold any outstanding stock in the business and whether these will pose difficulties for this new venture's viability.

Would a CEO of a business with a valuation of $50 million agree to a 50/50 merger with a company that earns $20k yearly and whose revenue is trending downward? It is unlikely as it would pose a significant financial risk for the larger business, as it would require an unequal investment with uncertain returns.

Secondly, the disparity in financial resources and performance suggests a potential mismatch in capabilities and strategic alignment, which could hinder the partnership's success. Additionally, the larger business may have concerns about the smaller business's ability to contribute equally in terms of commitment, expertise, and financial management, raising doubts about the feasibility of a truly equitable partnership.

Marriage and business share similarities in partnership, investment, and mutual benefit. Both require equal valuation, communication, shared goals, and pooling of strengths to thrive. The risks and uncertainties inherent can be mitigated by the stability and long-term perspective view of both partners. An equitable merger can ultimately yield immeasurable rewards, including emotional fulfillment, personal growth, and a sense of shared accomplishment.

History has shown that choosing a compatible spouse can significantly impact a man's professional trajectory. Through mutual encouragement, a woman's supportive qualities can translate into a warm home environment, reduced stress, and improved work ethic. In essence, a strong partnership can act as a foundation for success across various aspects of a man's life.

However, making the wrong decision in this regard could be costly. The legal system leans in favor of wives and mothers in divorce and custody proceedings. In the unfortunate event of a divorce, a man's happiness, assets, children, and even his freedom may all be at stake. Given the potential consequences, careful consideration is paramount. Therefore, it's imperative to meticulously assess any "Red Flags" to ensure they won't jeopardize future happiness and the relationship's longevity.

My Son... Please understand that this partnership, this marriage, means joining yourself to another for as long as you both shall live. Please know that this woman will be your most intimate confidant, and if things ever get complicated, she will help you seek a solution rather than "burn down the house" on her way out. The one who will be by your side through sickness and health will bear and help raise your children—the one who is equally invested in the marriage and will always seek her husband's best interest. Selecting the right woman for this partnership is the most critical decision you will ever make. It is one decision that you can't get wrong.

Choose wisely.

10 STEPS FOR SUCCESS

1. NEVER BE CONTROLLED BY SEX, MONEY OR A SUBSTANCE
2. KEEP YOUR BODY FIT AND EAT HEALTHY EVERYDAY
3. TRAVEL BEFORE SETTLING DOWN
4. NEVER CHASE AND NEVER EVER SHOW DESPERATION
5. FOR EVERY 1 MAN THERE ARE 10 WOMEN IN THE WORLD - DON'T SETTLE
6. NEVER MOVE IN WITH A WOMAN - OWN YOUR OWN RESIDENCE
7. NEVER STAY IN A RELATIONSHIP WHERE YOU'RE NOT RESPECTED
8. EXAMINE HER FAMILY AND UPBRINGING - YOU'LL FIND OUT A LOT
9. MAKE SURE SHE IS INVESTED EQUALLY IN THE RELATIONSHIP
10. WHEN YOU FIND THE ONE - LOVE AND CHERISH HER FOREVER

OF COURSE, A MAN SHOULD BE CONQUERING HIS OWN "RED FLAGS" BUT THAT'S ANOTHER STORY.

NOTES

I hope this book has provided valuable insights for your journey to marriage. Your feedback is highly valued, both positive and constructive. Please take a moment to share your experience online.

Thanks

A. Lamar

www.ingramcontent.com/pod-product-compliance
Lightning Source LLC
LaVergne TN
LVHW051601080426
835510LV00020B/3091